Can the Mind Be Quiet?

Can the Mind Be Quiet?

LIVING, LEARNING & MEDITATION

JIDDU KRISHNAMURTI

ALEPH

ALEPH BOOK COMPANY
An independent publishing firm
promoted by *Rupa Publications India*

Published in India in 2023
by Aleph Book Company
7/16 Ansari Road, Daryaganj
New Delhi 110 002

Copyright © 2023 Krishnamurti Foundation Trust, Ltd.
Cover image: Wikimedia Commons

Krishnamurti Foundation Trust Ltd.,
Brockwood Park, Bramdean, Hampshire
SO24 0LQ, England.
E-mail: info@kfoundation.org
Website: www.kfoundation.org

For further information about J. Krishnamurti please visit:
www.jkrishnamurti.org

All rights reserved.

The author has asserted his moral rights.

The views and opinions expressed in this book are the author's own and the facts are as reported by him, which have been verified to the extent possible, and the publishers are not in any way liable for the same.

No part of this publication may be reproduced, transmitted, or stored in a retrieval system, in any form or by any means, without permission in writing from Aleph Book Company.

ISBN: 978-93-95853-21-7

1 3 5 7 9 10 8 6 4 2

For sale in the Indian subcontinent only.

Printed in India.

This book is sold subject to the condition that it shall not, by way of trade or otherwise, be lent, resold, hired out, or otherwise circulated without the publisher's prior consent in any form of binding or cover other than that in which it is published.

CONTENTS

Explorations with Krishnamurti viii
Foreword ix

PART ONE
EXPLORATIONS INTO LIVING

1. We do not see, we do not hear — 3
2. How can the centre end? — 7
3. The stream of life — 10
4. Ignorance of oneself is the cause of conflict — 13
5. Why do we divide the outer and the inner? — 17
6. Conflict in any form is destruction of energy — 20
7. How do I bring up my children? — 26
8. What can stop degeneration in the world? — 30
9. You have made the mind a slave to words — 32
10. Pleasure soon becomes pain — 35
11. Comparison breeds discontent — 38
12. What brings about perception? — 43
13. Can my child's brain cells be changed? — 46
14. Choice exists only when the mind is confused — 50
15. Control in any form is distortion — 55
16. Solitude means freedom — 59
17. Can the mind unburden itself? — 62
18. We take a wrong turn and get lost — 69
19. The intellect is very limited — 73
20. The positive approach is destructive — 77
21. Life cannot be ruled by ideas — 80
22. Is creation different from expression? — 83
23. How we waste our life! — 85
24. All seeking is from emptiness and fear — 88
25. Can I stop decline in myself? — 93

26.	At what depth do you want order?	96
27.	Wisdom does not come through practice	100
28.	The brain needs complete security	105
29.	Intense watchfulness	112

PART TWO
EXPLORATIONS INTO LEARNING

30.	Education is to bring about the extraordinary beauty of order	117
31.	Teach through dialogue rather than merely impart knowledge	123
32.	To learn cooperation is part of education	129
33.	Thought divides	134
34.	The intellect can never be free	139
35.	Knowledge is detrimental to learning	145
36.	Knowledge is static	150
37.	Knowledge becomes an impediment to relationship	155
38.	Freedom from the known is the highest intelligence	160
39.	Sex becomes an obsessive god	165
40.	What does virtue mean?	172
41.	Only the undistorted mind can see truth	178

PART THREE
EXPLORATIONS INTO MEDITATION

42.	What really is sacred?	185
43.	Choiceless awareness and attention	189
44.	Why do you meditate?	192
45.	The religious mind is the meditative mind	195
46.	Opinion is not truth	199
47.	Meditation is intelligence	202
48.	Meditation is the essence of energy	205
49.	Life is an extraordinarily beautiful movement	212
50.	What is it to be aware?	217
51.	The strange sense of otherness	229

52.	Meditation is to see the fact of distortion	231
53.	We don't see the whole	233
54.	Meditation is the movement of great sensitivity	235
55.	Can the brain ever be quiet?	238
56.	Love is not an abstraction	241
57.	Meditation is emptying the mind of word and symbol	243
58.	The ending of time is the ending of change	245
59.	Thought cannot empty the mind	247
60.	Silence	250

EXPLORATIONS WITH KRISHNAMURTI

Along with Krishnamurti's public talks, his dialogues with leading 20th-century thinkers such as Renee Weber, Iris Murdoch, Jonas Salk, David Bohm and Huston Smith are well known. In between these hundreds of meetings, Krishnamurti was also available for private interviews and conversations with those who wished to meet him. These were not recorded and note-taking was discouraged.

Compiled here are sixty such conversations, previously unpublished, recalled and written down by Krishnamurti in the late 1960s and early 1970s. They contain probing inquiries into such topics as the self and consciousness, the essential qualities of good education, and the meditative and religious mind. As with all of his writings, the style is direct, eschews rhetoric and states deep truths as obvious and factual information, available to any who will listen. The pieces also include Krishnamurti's much-loved descriptions of nature.

The book is divided into three parts, representing far-reaching explorations into the areas of living, learning and meditation, highlighting Krishnamurti's radical approach to each.

FOREWORD

I met Krishnamurti for the first time in Rome in 1968, while I was working on a movie with Federico Fellini, the great Italian director. I spoke no Italian, so he had given me an interpreter, who also happened to be his personal astrologer. One day she said to me, 'You've been invited to a lunch with Krishnamurti.'

I said, 'Who's Krishnamurti?'

She then replied, in a hushed voice, as if I should know, 'Well...you know...he's Krishnamurti.'

I asked, 'Okay, is he a film director?'

'No no,' she said, 'he's a sage.'

Now I was 27 and famous, but really I am just an East End spiv and right then I was winging it. The only sage that I knew of went in the stuffing that my mother made at home for our roast dinners. All the same, I was interested enough to go along to this lunch party. It was only years later that I found out how I actually came to be there.

Fellini had an amazing script that he wanted to shoot. However he was short of money, so he asked Vanda Scaravelli, the eminent yoga teacher and well-connected society figure, for assistance. She knew Krishnamurti, and Fellini asked to be introduced to him next time he was in Rome, thinking I suppose that he might provide some funding.

A few months later Krishnamurti was in town, and she arranged for them to meet. Hearing that he loved movies, Fellini cut together about 15 minutes of the rushes of the film that he and I were making. He then showed it to him to break the ice, and apparently, when the short film finished, Krishnamurti said 'I'd like to meet that boy' (meaning me), which was why I was invited to lunch.

When I arrived the place was crowded, but I still ended up at a table opposite Krishnamurti himself. We didn't speak at all. But, because I was staring at him, he continually lowered his eyes out of politeness. I remember thinking that I had never met anybody like that. It was very unusual. Then after the lunch he was answering questions from the press people there and his secretary Alain Naudé came over to me and said, 'Would you like to go for a walk with Krishnamurti?' I said yes.

So he and I went out for this long walk around the suburbs of Rome. And not having had the nerve to speak with him during lunch, I suddenly couldn't stop chattering. At a certain point on the walk we stopped and he put his hand on my arm and said, 'Look at that tree.' And I looked—it was a tree. I looked at him. He smiled. I smiled. We carried on walking. I carried on talking. Ten minutes later he stopped me again and said, 'Look at that cloud.' And I looked—again, cloud. It wasn't special, not lit from within or anything like that: it was a cloud, that's all. On we went, and I kept talking.

And that was my first meeting with Krishnaji. However, I was never the same after that meeting. Something shifted. He did something to me, which I understood years later: he used his presence to pause my own thinking. And something inside started reaching back out towards me.

From then on, every time I saw that he was giving a talk, I would try and go, and likewise he would always try and make sure that I was invited. I often wouldn't really get what was being said, but unbeknownst to me I was being refined. In later conversations the same thing would happen: we would start off talking about material things like shirts and shoes, and yet a shift would occur. His tone of voice would not necessarily change, but something subtle would take place. I can only liken it to Cole Porter's lyric, 'How strange the change from major to minor.' It took me maybe 15 years to understand sayings like: 'When the eagle flies it leaves no mark,' and 'The observer is the observed.'

I might not have been sure about what he was saying, but there was always this shift.

Terence Stamp

PART ONE

EXPLORATIONS INTO LIVING

1

WE DO NOT SEE, WE DO NOT HEAR

The north wind blew hard and cold, wiping away the fog, the smell of the town, the exhaust and the foul air. The mountains were very clear. The air was brittle, sweeping everything before it—the dead and dying leaves. You could see very far to the gap between the islands and you could almost see every bush and every leaf on the hill. That strange light that exists only in California was more penetrating than ever. You really should see these hills in this light, with the blue sky beyond them, and then you would know the extraordinary beauty of the land. The sun was on the sea, this morning one vast sheet of silver. It was good to look at the light of the water and let that light enter into your heart, and to live there with that light and nothing else, with no thought, without tomorrow or yesterday, and to let the north wind blow away all the inanities, the ugliness, the violence and the stupidities that man has built into himself by his own thought and fear. Let all that be swept away and have that light and nothing else.

'You have often said be nothing, completely destroy everything, the good and the bad, and withdraw into silence, into nothingness. Aren't you really teaching total annihilation of the ego and all the works of the ego? You are really saying to people, live a life of nothingness and from that nothingness act. This is what the Bhagavad-Gita or the Upanishads say in their own way: complete and total annihilation of the "me", the ego, the super-ego. How is this to be done? Does it come about through meditation or through good work? Is it a reward for righteous behaviour? How does it happen?'

There are two kinds of action. One brings you reward, and the doing of it strengthens the ego, the 'me'. The other kind of action, the action which you love to do, has no reward or punishment and is not concerned with what the neighbour says, or with gods or with the priests or with belief. You do it because it is the only thing to do. You rejoice in the very doing of it, not for heaven or the avoidance of hell. You just do it and in the very doing of it is the delight. This action is of freedom from society and has nothing whatsoever to do with morality. This action is from nothingness. When there is this, you can look at the world from that silence of nothingness.

You ask how this happens. Thought can only go as far as its own distance and dimension, for it is tethered. Thought, however bright, clear, perceptive, is still part of the known, and the known is not that nothingness. Thought cannot destroy the known, for it is itself the already known. But thought must exercise itself to its fullest width and height and see its own barren activity. Neither is it through organised meditation, for as long as there is the meditator, meditation is within the field of the known. What is important is the ending of the meditator. So it is not organised meditation with its systems, methods and goals, nor is it the pursuit and refinement of thought. It is the clear eye that sees and the clear heart that hears. The hearing and seeing of the ego is one thing, the seeing and hearing without the ego is another. The one perverts and distorts, the other simply sees and hears. This hearing is from the silence of nothingness. The total denial is the total action.

'May I ask you what actually is the action of that denial? Is it to see something in the mind that is false and to somehow say no to it? If it is, then there is something saying the no. That cannot be what you mean, so what is the quality of that denial?'

There is no 'me' when you deny because the 'me' has already been denied.

'But to most of us denial implies a seeing of something and a rejection of it.'

Denial is the seeing and the doing, not two separate things.

'But what is this doing that you speak of? I understand there has to be seeing, a perception of something, but having seen that what is this action?'

There is no action. The seeing itself is the denying.

'Do you mean that if you see something there is no alternative, there is no wrong, there is no other than seeing?'

That's just it. We divide action from seeing and we ask what the action is that comes about in the seeing. The seeing itself is action; there is no actor in the seeing. If there is an actor in the seeing there is no seeing at all, and no hearing when there is one who hears.

'You seem to be describing a quality of seeing and hearing at a far more profound level than most human beings can even imagine.'

I don't think it is so very profound, I think it's fairly clear and simple. Hearing or seeing without the observer, without the one who hears and translates; just the act of seeing and listening and nothing else.

'But may I suggest that for most of us the act of seeing is hedged about by the limitations of the person. It's as though you are saying that in order to sweep all that away one must see, and we do not see because we are confined by these qualities.'

We are confined by the 'me', by the ego or the super-ego.

'But are you not saying that the seeing and the hearing that you describe sweeps away the ego and the "me"?'

Yes, but one has to be aware of the ego, the 'me' that is interfering with the seeing; and to be aware without any choice is the seeing. The moment you choose what you want to hear or what you want to see, all the mischief of acting with a motive or with a desire or for pleasure begins.

'May I then ask you if it could be like this: one observes

something and one must at the same time observe all the action that immediately comes into play through the ego and through thought, so that one is seeing the objective thing and also the whole subjective mechanism in the mind all at once?'

Surely, surely. First of all, we don't see, we really don't hear. We hear and see with the limitation, the conditioning of the ego, of the 'me'—the 'me' being the society, the fear and so on. One must realise the fact that one does not see, one does not hear. When one recognises that fact you move to a different level.

'Trying to follow you through this I am immediately aware of all these things. Are you suggesting that seeing them, as it were, in a mass, in a clump, as a fact, one then moves past them and is free of them? Or is it necessary to say, "Yes, I see this, this, this and this..."?'

No, no. One must see it as a whole and put it away as a whole. The seeing it as a whole is the ending of it.

'But this is a very dangerous thing because the mind caught in thought is apt to say, "Yes, there is the factor of conditioning, there is the factor of thought, I see it"—and not really see it. It takes it as a cipher.'

That is a pretension, that is a vanity of a sense of seeing. We have made it very clear that seeing or hearing is not possible when there is any interpretation, when there is any attachment.

'Yes, the quality of this is so totally other than what we do almost all of the time.'

2

HOW CAN THE CENTRE END?

The mountains were full of solitude. It had been raining off and on for three days and the mountains were green with light. They had become almost blue, and in their fullness they were making the heavens rich and beautiful. There was great silence, unlike the sea; when you walked on the beach in the wet sand, the breakers made a great deal of noise. There was no silence there except in your heart. But among the mountains on that winding path, silence was everywhere. The noise of the town, the roar of the traffic and the thunder of the waves could not be heard. It was a beautiful afternoon, and with the setting sun a few of the hilltops seemed to be alive with a light of their own.

'One is always puzzled about action, and it gets more and more bewildering when one sees the complexity of life. There are so many things that should be done and there are other things that need immediate action. The world around us is changing so rapidly—its values, its morality, its wars and peace—that one is utterly lost before the immediacy of action. Yet one is always asking oneself what one should do, confronted with the enormous problem of living. One has lost one's faith in most things—in the leaders, in the teachers, in beliefs—and one often wishes for some kind of principle that operates in spite of oneself, something that would light your path, or some authority that would tell you what to do. But we also know in our heart that all these things are something dead and gone. Yet invariably we come back, asking ourselves what it is all about and what we are to do in this.'

As one observes, we have always acted from a centre which

contracts and expands. Sometimes it is a very small circle and at other times it is comprehensive, inclusive and utterly satisfying. But it is always a centre of grief and sorrow, of fleeting joys and misery, the enchanting or the painful past. It is a centre which most of us know, consciously or unconsciously. From the centre we act and we have our roots in it. The question of what to do, now or tomorrow, is always asked from this centre, and the reply must always be recognisable by the centre. Having received a reply, either from another or from ourselves, we proceed to act according to the limitation of the centre. It is like an animal tethered to a post, its action depending on the length of the rope. This action is never free and so there is always pain, mischief and confusion. Realising this, the centre says to itself, 'How am I to be free to live happily, completely openly, and act without sorrow or remorse?' But it is still the centre that is asking the question.

This centre is the past. This centre is the 'me' with its self-centred activities, which only knows action in terms of reward and punishment, of achievement and failure, with motives, causes and effects. It is caught in this chain. This chain is the centre and the prison.

There is the other action that comes when there is space in which there is no centre, a dimension in which there is no cause and effect. From this, living is action. Having no centre, whatever is done is free, joyous, without the pain of pleasure. This space and freedom is not a result of effort and achievement: when the centre ends the other is.

'But how can the centre end? What am I to do to end it? What disciplines, what sacrifices, what great efforts have I to make?'

None. Only see without any choice the activities of the centre; not as an observer, not as an outsider looking within, but just observe without the censor.

'I can't do it, I am always looking with the eyes of the past.'

Then be aware that you're looking with the eyes of the past and be with it. Remain with it; don't try to do anything about it. Be simple and know that whatever you try to do is the response of your own desire to escape from it and will only strengthen the centre. So there is no escape, no effort and no despair. Then you can see the full meaning of the centre and the immense danger of it.

3

THE STREAM OF LIFE

He was a tall man, well dressed, with rather sharp eyes. He had studied Buddhism as it promised intellectual nourishment and he liked the Buddhist outlook on life. Although he was born a Christian, there was no meaning in Christianity except service in the love of God, helping man to become more helpless. Even Buddhism did not satisfy him and so he had left that too, although he was vaguely playing with one philosophical outlook or another, or some vague teacher or another. But his mind was keen, alert, questioning and exploring. He sat in the armchair rather comfortably, his legs crossed. His shoes were well polished. You can tell a great deal from the hands. He had rather stubby but fine hands. He said he did a great deal of gardening and took delight in flowers, and kept his lawn free of dandelions and weeds. He said he had a large house, a wife but no children. From his description of the house, it must have been nice, full of old furniture and with clean polished floors. He seemed to like good food. One wondered why he was telling all this.

The room was very pleasant with a green carpet and lovely curtains. It overlooked a green lawn and a magnificent tulip tree which had blossomed so beautifully with large flowers in the early summer. On the left was a magnificent cedar, old and ready to die. Beyond the lawn was a field and a grove, copses and fields. It was a pleasant place and peaceful, undisturbed by passing traffic. There was great beauty and stillness. You really could feel the earth. There were trees all around, old, heavy with leaves, beautiful in shape. That evening they were casting long shadows. It was delightful to watch them and as you watched, the whole earth changed. Everything seemed alive and you were part of it, not only on the hard chair but out there, part of the throbbing beauty and stillness. You were not identifying yourself with them; it was not an intellectual process of identification but, rather, you were of them. They were your friends. Their whispers were your whispers and their movement was part of your mind and heart. It was not imagination either, for that can play tricks on you, deceiving you with fantasies, oversensitive reactions and false flights into emotional states called love. It was none of these things. There was no separation between you, the earth and the heavens and the trees. The colours of the green lawn and the deep shadows were the colours of your mind and heart. Yellow doesn't aspire to greater yellowness. The green lawn was so fantastically alive in the evening light that every part of you was of it. A pheasant walked across the lawn and you went with it, disappearing behind a bush.

The man said, 'I came to this morning's meeting and the others. A stream goes by my house, a pleasant, shadowy stream. It wanders through many pools which I have dug, but the main stream goes by. I have dug others and that is my work. Two or three times a week I do other kinds of work to add to my little income. But I seem to be stuck. I don't quite know what is the matter with me. I can think, I can argue fairly clearly and cleverly. I have read a good deal but all this seems so utterly empty and my life seems to have come to a stop. Even the flowers and the green lawn I keep so carefully is losing its delight.'

There is the stream that goes through your place, on and on and on, and you have dug little pools into which the water comes and remains for the lilies to grow. You are a bit like that, aren't you, living in the little pools, comfortable, avoiding danger, satisfied? And that stream goes by, and the stream is life.

'Yes, I see what you mean. That is exactly what I've done.

How strange you spotted it so quickly.'

He was quiet for a while, looking at me, surprised and rather taken aback. Presently he said, 'What have I to do now?'

The room was full of silence and his question went round in the silence. He was finding his own answer. He couldn't quite make it and so he asked the same question: 'How is one to let go of the little pools that one has dug for oneself, that garden, the house, the books, the furniture and the wife, and enter into the stream and flow with it endlessly?'

A river flows over every obstacle, for it has great volume of water behind it. It may form little pools and sluggish backwaters but it is the river forming them, and in the rainy season they will all be washed away by the greater volume of water. The river is always flowing, past the rocks, the islands, the fields. The river is inexhaustible, so is life.

'Must I let go,' he asked, 'of my little pools which I have carefully dug, my lawn and the trees?'

There is no answer to this question. There is the lovely stream with shadows and swiftly flowing current, and the pools, some rich and some stagnant. There is no 'how', for if you ask how then you will never leave the pools, the house and the garden. You will always be sitting on the bank watching the stream go by. There is never any 'how', only the act of entering the stream and flowing with it endlessly.

4

IGNORANCE OF ONESELF IS THE CAUSE OF CONFLICT

'What is conflict? I have read many of your books and I think I'm sufficiently able to go into things, into myself, into the complexities of relationship. I am also aware of the world around me and the social injustice. I have studied Vedanta and I think I can understand things intellectually and actually. I have discussed religious subjects with many people all over the world, with scholars and with students. If I may say so, I think I have a fairly sharp brain, and when I ask what conflict is, it is not that I want a definition or a panacea to solve all conflict. I am asking because it seems to me that all life is conflict, all relationship is conflict, everything one does and doesn't do is a stress and strain. There is the temperamental conflict between two human beings, conflict of character, conflict of intentions, conflict of will and desire. There is the conflict of frustration, thwarted hopes, the conflict of confusion—not being able to cope with oneself or with a situation. So there is the conflict of our daily living and also there are the deep-rooted conflicts of which one is only darkly aware. This strife is overwhelming, apparently inevitable, and yet one struggles against it. There is the strife of the sane and the strife of the neurotic. All life is a battle. Some of the conflicts arise from deep-seated tendencies either inherited or acquired, the result of temperament or conditioning.'

Can we say that most of our conflicts, whether of temperament or character or acquired, are the result of conditioning? Is all conflict the outcome of our limited perception, our limited understanding of ourselves? Would you say that in understanding ourselves conflict will come to an end? Or is conflict something over which we have no control at all? And if it is beyond our capacity to come to grips with it, is there any problem at all? Is conflict ignorance? There is the fact of conflict and there are a thousand explanations and descriptions of its varieties. And then we have the question: can anything be done about it? What is conflict? When are you aware of it?

'One is aware of it when it hurts, or when there is a demand for more pleasure.'

Are you aware of conflict all the time or only sometimes?

'Only sometimes.'

Why only sometimes? What is going on when you are not aware of it? Are you daydreaming, occupied with other things, escaping into something, being entertained?

'When I am not aware of it, there is no conflict, or rather when there is no conflict I am not aware of that.'

So you are only aware of it when there is conflict. Conflict makes you aware of its existence, through pain and so on. It isn't, of course, that the awareness makes the conflict! So what is taking place when there is no conflict? When the mind is totally absorbed by something and occupied, in that state there is no conflict. That is what we all want, something that will absorb us so that we can forget ourselves. But the conflict is only in abeyance—it is still there and comes up as strong as ever when the occupation ceases. So we demand to be occupied with something all the time. More and more we make sure that we are occupied so that the conflict which is always round the corner doesn't show its head. The mind is like a child absorbed by an intricate toy. As long as the toy holds interest, the child is absorbed by it; when the toy is broken or taken away the child cries. That is what is happening with us. When we are not absorbed by the occupation we are occupied with the conflict itself. Whatever it is that occupies us— career, political or social activity, sex, entertainment, God or the state—we will defend these things at all costs because we are frightened to face this conflict which is always there. So we are either occupied with the occupation or occupied with the conflict; and occupation brings again its own conflicts.

So there are these three points: there is absorption by a 'toy', being absorbed by a conflict, and thirdly both these things are resistance to that state of mind which is empty, fear of that state of mind which is not occupied at all. The petty, shallow mind wants to be absorbed by the toy or by its own conflict. The conflict is self-concern, and absorption by the toy is apparent non-self-concern. But the self-concern and the apparent non-self-concern are both the same. The understanding of these three things is the understanding of oneself. It is the ignorance of oneself that is the cause of conflict.

'Are you saying that the understanding of these things, which is the understanding of the very nature of oneself, is the ending of conflict?'

When you understand yourself, conflict ends. So conflict is ignorance of the design in which it exists, and the very design is its very existence. Seeing this nonverbally is to end it.

'Do you mean to say that I must not be occupied with anything?'

You can be occupied and yet not be absorbed by that occupation. If you are occupied with a motive of which you are not aware then you are resisting conflict, though that fact may be hidden. But if you give attention to what you are doing, that attention is not engendered by the conflict hidden round the corner, from which you are escaping. Attention is without motive.

'If I do something I enjoy, isn't this enjoyment the motive?'

If you love to do something you enjoy it. In that there is no conflict. Enjoyment is the beauty of this love. If you do something for its own sake, for the love of it, there is no motive and therefore no conflict. Enjoyment therefore is not a sin. But the fear of losing enjoyment is again conflict. The measure of the mind is conflict: loss, gain and fulfilment. So one asks oneself whether the mind can be in a state of attention, and therefore of love, not absorbed by anything.

'The surfer enjoying a wonderful wave with all his heart and the child playing with a toy, aren't they both absorbed?'

Of course they are.

'Yet you say to do something with love and enjoyment is intelligent, is different from being absorbed.'

You possess, dominate, hold on to the thing that absorbs you, and when that is gone you are back again with your tears, like the child. The man who enjoys what he is doing is not possessed by what he is doing. The man who loves is anonymous. The man who possesses is clamorous; for him there is conflict, and not for the other. The important thing in all this is not being possessed by that which occupies you. Freedom is the ending of conflict. When you are attached there is pain. Knowing that you say, 'I must be detached,' and this attempt to become detached is conflict, which is the same as being attached.

5

WHY DO WE DIVIDE
THE OUTER AND THE INNER?

They had just arrived at the railway station. They were garlanded. They were dressed in homespun cottons known as khadi and these, with the sandals and caps they always seemed to wear, were their badge. Nonviolence was on their lips. They worked for the liberation of the land, had been to prison for many years, suffered for the cause, and when the foreign power left they were the cream of the land. Most of them were Brahmins and Gandhi was their leader. They everlastingly talked about nonviolence but they were violent people. They believed it was necessary to be non-worldly but all their actions were worldly, political, social. They had all the gestures of humility but were arrogant. They followed the successful because in their hearts they were failures. They had a holy dread of sex and some of them had taken vows of celibacy, yet they were surrounded by girls. They pursued peace and yet they were extraordinarily tortured human beings. They were traditional though they were familiar with the modern Western writers and their ideas; they knew the scriptures and the modern philosophers. There was a contradiction between the scientific world and the religious world. They identified with the poor and were familiar with the powerful. They talked of the villages where they were the leaders, harbingers of enlightenment and hope. Simple of appearance in their white clothes, inwardly they were tortured human beings, confused, deeply marked, miserable.

In 1948 they were the heroes of this struggle and the custodians of the future which promised bright before them.

They had the highest hopes for their land and everybody believed they would usher in a new golden age. Today they are lost, useless, failures; burned-out. All their fire, enthusiasm and eagerness has gone. They are tired, disillusioned and lead a pointless life, isolated, though talking, gesturing and writing. They are very clever people and can discourse for hours persuasively, but they are lost, bitter, unhappy, lonely. They are like people anywhere else who have committed themselves to a particular course of action which they hope will lead to success at the end of it. With success or without success they are emptyhanded and empty of heart. They are full of other people's knowledge and have very little of their own. This is not a cruel exaggeration. The picture is a sad one for all of us because all of us belong in some way or other to this group of mankind.

What went wrong, what has happened? Why is it that, knowing everything that books, experience and the writings of the saints can teach, they have learned nothing and are utterly lost? We are the same. This is not a criticism of a particular group; through this group we see every group and through these people we see ourselves. Most of us are lost, unhappy, lonely, bitter.

I think it is right to ask now, seeing all this, not only how to prevent this dreadful disease from spreading but also what to do with it in our own hearts. This urge to do something outwardly, to reform, to change, to organise improvement, is the first symptom of this fatal disease. The other fatal symptom is the opposite of the first: saying that everything is in me and I must change first. This division is the cause of the disease. One can never separate the outer and the inner. The violence and disorder out there is the violence and disorder inside: the two are the same indivisibly.

Their nonviolence was only a slogan, a political instrument of the violence inside. There was compulsion, rigid discipline, conformity to a brutal pattern of what they considered morality. There was always in them this cruel conflict to conform to what they considered the highest virtue, and this was their own invention. They also forced others to conform to their pattern. They were essentially traditionalists and therefore contradictory.

Why do we divide the outer and the inner? Is it because we cannot control the outer that we hope to control and change the inner? Is it part of our intellectual escape from what we really are? We do not see that we are the result of the past. Without dying to the past in ourselves, we must inevitably follow the path of tradition which has made both the outer and the inner. The outer and the inner are interlocked and determine each other. Both are changed when the past is denied. Denying the past in our own hearts, we deny it also in our actions which are the outer.

So what have you and I to do in order not to degenerate into hopeless tortured human beings? Is there anything positive we can do at all? If you do anything positive it will be in the line of tradition. But if you deny tradition you have already done the most radical thing and change has already taken place.

Degeneration takes place when past habit, which is tradition and your particular idiosyncrasy borne out of the past, is pursued. Wherever there is continuity in conforming to a conceptual pattern of life—whether that concept is traditional, orthodox or particular, projected by your own desire, inclination and hope—there is decline and a meaningless life. To invent a meaningful life, however noble or clever, is the same as following somebody else's meaning. So we see degeneration and understand its whole structure. This seeing is understanding and is not an intellectual act. This is energy which is not acting against itself. Be aware of all this in action, in living and in all relationships.

6

CONFLICT IN ANY FORM IS DESTRUCTION OF ENERGY

It was a long, hot journey. Dust poured into the carriages and covered everything. The compartment didn't give much shelter from the sun and the dust. It was crowded; people came in at different stations with their bags, the porters and the loud talk. It got hotter and hotter as we went and the train got later and later.

It was a beautiful country with rivers, palm trees and tamarind. Early in the morning villagers drove their cattle to where there might possibly be some green things to eat. The hills with their big boulders were brilliant against the blue sky. The villagers would work for hours in the fields using wooden ploughs and driving their oxen which would labour, bellowing, in the hot sun.

The train stopped at a station where vendors noisily set out fruit and sweetmeats covered with flies. Everyone seemed bothered and hot. Presently there was a hoot and the train began to move. In the cool of the evening the train stopped for an hour. The guard said that we were held up by another train that was also late. Looking out of the window one saw a man covered with dust and ashes practising yoga. He was doing various asanas, standing on his head, sitting in the lotus position, doing the complicated exercises with such ease and grace that people were throwing him coins. The yogic practices were done extra well with great skill and consummate ease, all for a few pennies. Probably he did this every day. He was very thin, rather ascetic looking. He was doing his exercises in the dust even though he had swept clean the earth on which he was showing off. It was rather sad. Probably he could have earned a great deal of money, but in that field there was much competition. Not being educated properly and with no one to help him, he would never leave that village but gather daily a little money to eat, and if he had a family, to feed them. A black goat went by with heavy horns. A cow came along and lay in the shade of a tree. Everything seemed so peaceful; the vendors had gone and the train was waiting.

A fellow passenger was eating a banana and reading a sacred book. He never looked out of the window during that hour, never saw the poor yogi, dirty and worn out. He never saw the hills, the deepening shadows, the cows coming home in the dust and the village women gathering around the water tap. He thought he was engrossed in religious matters for he was reading aloud to himself, but the beauty of the land lay outside and not in the voice which came across the little space in that compartment. It was rather sad, that emaciated yogi and this fat little man proudly reading his book, and the cow sleeping in the shade. It all seemed so utterly without love, without any feeling.

Suddenly the monkeys came; the long-tailed, black-faced, grey-haired ones. They were quite big and there were many of them. They sat among the trees, looking down at all the things happening around the station, silently, totally indifferent and still. They had come from the hills. They were not town dwellers so they were healthy, extraordinarily graceful. The little ones were playful, dancing up and down, and every movement was a joy. It was a great delight to watch them and the whole earth seemed to rejoice in their stillness, their playfulness and their grace. One could hear the other train coming and the monkeys shot away. They disappeared and with them went the beauty and the quiet of that evening, until the stars came. The rattling train never shattered the peace of the night. The stars seemed so close, so brilliant. It was extraordinary, the feel of the earth and the stars and to have no space between them and you.

You were not aware of the stillness and the beauty of it. If you were, it wouldn't be there. Because you were not, so it was there with the monkeys and the yogi and the fat man with his prayers.

'I am a bachelor, though I have had affairs. I don't take them very seriously but they have eaten a great part of my life. I have wasted a great deal of energy fighting, yielding, being passionate and then being merely routine. I have always felt that I needed a great deal of energy to live, to resist, to discipline, to be free. I was in a monastery where there were monks with their routine, their cruel discipline and their denial of the flesh—although they ate a great deal of meat. They thought they needed energy to devote their lives to God; like the communists who are vigorously committed to a dialectic ideology with their own brutal discipline and dedicated lives— they too needed energy. And there is the wandering monk, the sannyasi, who in denying the world hopes to have immense energy which will carry him towards reality. A factory worker also needs energy to do the monotonous daily movements following a machine. Everyone, from the highly privileged to the lowest of human beings, all need driving energy.'

Every human being needs energy to do anything. There is the energy that comes through friction, through conflict, through hate and violence. There is the energy that comes through action, through resistance, through contention; the greater the contention and conflict, the greater the energy. If you have a gift as a writer or for politics, the greater the ambition, the greater the drive. To go to an office every day, with the boredom, the little excitement, the control of others, all this demands energy, perseverance, a sustained drive. The monk in his cell with his vows, resisting every form of natural demand, cultivates a peculiar energy that sustains him in his belief and in his activities. This energy is a form of violence. Religions throughout the world have maintained that to reach the highest you must not dissipate sexual energy but that energy must be dedicated to God and so serve mankind. This abstinence is regarded as holy, although in the West it is breaking down and priests and bishops are beginning to marry. The ultimate wastage of energy is war and the preparation for war with the instruments of war.

'I know this, at least some of it, but how are we to control this wastage, this spending of energy on things that don't matter, and focus on essentials?'

Before we go into that, we must clearly understand what is the real wastage and not spend our time being concerned with what is essential and what is not. In that there is duality and the conflict between the opposites which is spending of energy and is not creative. So let us be concerned with understanding the enormous wastage of energy that we human beings indulge in. It is wasted in pursuit of ideologies and so avoiding what is. *It is wasted in daydreaming and in the images that one has built about oneself; in the pictures of pleasures, sensuous, sexual or so called spiritual; in the grudges that one bears; in the memorable pleasures that one keeps locked in the privacy of one's own mind; in the self-concern with all one's little problems and private quarrels with oneself and others; in the assumptions, the formulas, the opinions and the judgements. All these are a great waste of energy.*

'I think I understand what you mean by wastage. I am beginning to see clearly what is implied, what the implications are in all this, but I'm still concerned with controlling and directing the energy that is being so wasted. What am I to do?'

This desire to control is another form of wastage, for in that there is conflict, the controller separated from the thing controlled, the decision, the exertion of will and the constant struggle to overcome and put an end to wastage. All this implies duality; and the basic dissipation of energy is to think or feel in terms of duality, for the very nature of thought is fragmentation.

'But I am faced with this. I think in terms of duality. I have the pleasure of sex and the appetite for it. The thoughts and the pictures must obviously end, otherwise they just go on chewing over the past. I intellectually understand what you are talking about but the fact is I am not capable of putting an end to it. What am I to do?'

Does one really see that the opposing and contradictory desires, energies are a dissipation? Why do we have duality at all? There is only what is. The opposition is a resistance to what is. This resistance is the opposite and so there is conflict. Is it possible to be aware of what is *without resisting it?*

'But what if *what is* seems utterly stupid? How am I to change it?'

Do not create a conflict about the stupidity. Do not say it must be different, that you must become very clever; just face the fact of stupidity. How do you know it is stupid? Because you have compared it to something that you consider not stupid? Or you have been told it is stupid? If you have not been told, is it stupid?

'It may *be* stupid. What then?'

The very word stupid *implies a duality, and so there is a resistance to* what is. *So can you look at* what is *without verbalisation? Can you look without the word that is associated with particular knowledge? What really concerns us is that conflict in any form is destructive of energy. If we really deeply understand this, not verbally or intellectually but with our hearts and minds, then we shall know the action of reaction without bringing into it any form of resistance or conflict of duality. We then come to something that is extraordinarily interesting: this constant movement of thought is a great waste of energy. To use thought to function when necessary is not a wastage. To exercise thought logically, wholly, heightens energy. When thought wanders in daydreams, in imagination, in conceptual activities, it decreases energy. So can the mind be silent without the movement of thought, but when action demands, exercise thought fully out of this silence? Then there is a greater abundance of energy heightened, made sensitive and intelligent. This action of thought is not separate from the silent mind and therefore does not breed duality.*

Silence is not the opposite of noise. Silence is the very essence of energy.

The religious mind is part of meditation. Meditation is when there is no meditation.

7

HOW DO I BRING UP MY CHILDREN?

It was autumn and the sun was coming through the windows. The winds had not yet begun and on these pleasant, warm sunny days the leaves were turning gently red, yellow and some of them purple. The skies were extraordinarily clear, soft blue, and very close to the earth. The clouds lay on the horizon and the land was happy. The shadows were long, heavy, and the grass that morning was covered with heavy dew. The beauty of the earth and the sky seemed to fill the air and there was a pleasant feeling of the past summer and the spring to come. And for these pleasant days one would probably pay with hard winter.

I do not know if you ever look at trees. Not with memories, imagination and knowledge but just look at them peacefully, quietly, without any reactions and resistance of the brain; just to observe, in which the observer has come to an end; just to see the tree, the green lawn and the many cows in the field; just to observe them. As you observe, the space that brings division seems to fade away and there is only observation and the joy of looking.

The man had bright eyes and a quick smile. He said, 'How do I bring up my children? What am I to do with them? I have five children. Three of them are bright, beautiful and full of promise. The other two are very emotional, very tender, very affectionate; they don't seem to fight, quarrel; they are still with that innocence that comes with childhood, full of curiosity. The three are very sharp, always questioning, fighting, quarrelling among themselves, pushing each other around. What am I to do with them? If I send those three to a school they will naturally learn a lot of things, they will pass exams, be moulded by the other children, by the teacher, by knowledge, by the environment of that particular school. And they will go to university and be swallowed up in the structure of society as it is. With regard to the other two, I'm so afraid that they will get wounded, hurt, and turn more and more inward, perhaps withdraw altogether and be treated as odd eccentrics. I don't know how far they will go in their studies. How am I to educate them, knowing the danger, the destructiveness of schools, the incredible insufficiency of universities and colleges, however much they may give them scientific knowledge, technological information and capacity? I don't want them to be destroyed. I really love my children. I look at them every day at breakfast and I come home especially to see them at lunch and dinner. I spend a great deal of time with them, watching over them, talking and playing with them, and I feel very close to them. They are going to face this danger of education, the competitive, ruthless world of ambition, success and all the brutality that is there. How can I help them to avoid all this?'

Can you really help them to avoid all this mad brutality and violence? Or can you educate them to meet all this intelligently?

'Yes, but how am I to give them this intelligence, help them to acquire the capacity, of which you speak so much, to observe themselves and the world; and themselves not separate from the world but themselves who *are* the world? How can I give—no, not give or help—make them see?'

If you send them to school, as you must inevitably, they will be influenced by other children who are conditioned as your children are. They will influence them deliberately or unknowingly. The teacher will influence them and they will begin to lose their sensitivity, their curiosity, their spirit of inquiry. They will be made mediocre and their way of life will fall into the pattern which society has set.

'I am afraid I will have to send them to school; I cannot

give them private tuition. It would be bad for them; they must meet and play with other children; and they will be influenced, shaped and broken. I really don't know what to do. My wife and I have talked about it a great deal and we don't seem to be able to see a way out of all this. Sometimes I regret having had children at all.

'At home, can I help them to withstand the influence of the school, of the other children, and also help them to be free of the influence of myself and my wife, so that they can go really freely, intelligently? They are already conditioned; they have their own peculiar qualities, inclinations, tendencies, their narrow characters, resistances and peculiar demands.'

They are conditioned and this conditioning is the result of many thousand years of influences. When you talk of freedom, freedom is only possible when there is an end to this influence. Be aware and be free of this conditioning; only then can the mind and heart be free.

Education is not only to give them information, and in the very giving of information, through discussion to awaken or cultivate intelligence. It is also, surely, for them to understand their own prejudices, inclinations and tendencies, which is their conditioning; and to give them opportunities to test out their conditioning and see the danger of it and to be unconditionally free of it. The whole cultivation of man is also part of education.

'But there are no such schools in the world. Nobody is really interested, in a deep sense, in the children; they haven't the time, the energy, the patience, or perhaps the love. So what am I to do? Where am I in all this? What am I to do with my children? At home, can I reason and discuss with them to help them to see how other children are influencing them? It seems to me that is all I can do. Or find a school that will not condition the child completely. Are there any such schools? It is a great problem and I have been thinking about it a great deal. I don't know where to turn.

'It seems to me,' he went on, 'that one must have such schools in every part of the world, and with a few of my friends perhaps I could start one. But it needs a lot of money, space, a building and so on, and we are not very rich people. So I am back again where I started. I really don't know what to do, how to educate them. I see how important it is to change the whole structure of the society in which I live, and it seems to me one must begin with the very young, educate them entirely differently, help them to change themselves and then perhaps the society. All this implies a lot of work, demanding a great deal of energy. I wish you would have some of these schools all over the world, not just in one or two places.'

The sun was getting brighter and the sky was deepening in blue. The birds had now gone away; as winter was approaching there were very few birds on the lawn. There was the pheasant, the rabbit and the pigeons. And as the culture demands, they will be hunted, killed.

The essence of intelligence is sensitivity.

8

WHAT CAN STOP DEGENERATION IN THE WORLD?

Why don't we realise that the house is burning? Not your house or my house, your personal property or another's, but *the* house, *the* property. Is it because we are too insensitive to be aware of the house—that it is your house, my house and the other man's house, wherever we are—that is burning? Is it because we have no feeling left anymore? Have all our feelings, deep passions been exhausted, wasted away, spent on things that are irrelevant? Have we become callous, having expended our energy, our sympathy, our affection, on things that have no value at all, and so now we are exhausted, worn out? Or is it because our eyes have never looked beyond our own little house, our own little concern, our own little protection? We have no faith anymore because we have given our faith, our trust, and it has been taken away and destroyed, so we are dull, indifferent.

Or is it because in ourselves—as human beings, not as a particular human being—we are empty, and we have tried to fill that emptiness with such trivialities as belief, opinion, judgements, with political, so-called religious, or artistic activities? The man who is empty of heart writes a great deal about love; the man who cannot see, or is unhappy, composes music on love and beauty. The artist, empty inwardly, has to express, put it on canvas. This emptiness and the feeling of utter, complete loneliness which is part of this emptiness, makes us do things both outwardly and inwardly, and the result of all that is that we become weary, bitter, or live in great despair.

When the house is actually burning, as it is—the vast house that man has built is crumbling, being destroyed—we either don't see it or do not have the capacity to put the fire out. We have no trust in another, nor have we trust in ourselves, confidence to rebuild, to bring a new world into being, because in ourselves we are empty. We discover we are the result of everything that man has been and we cannot get away from our past. We may revolt against it, take drugs, start new communities, start a new expression, but it is the same old weary, dull, empty feeling in a different direction. What will make us see the fire, put it out and in the very act of putting it out, build a world that is entirely different?

What can stop this degeneration that is going on all over the world? Can a real religious spirit stop it?—which is not the beliefs, the rituals, the organised propaganda called religion. Organised bureaucracies with their vested interests and power, position, with their hierarchical outlook, all this is not religion. When we lose the deep, inward sense of something that is sacred, holy, then every form of fragmentation, degeneration and destruction must come into being. Man apparently has lost completely this essential beauty. This essential beauty, this abiding energy is the only factor that can bring about a different world.

To observe—not intellectually formulate or verbally construct an image—that the world is burning, to actually see the degeneration with your mind, with your heart, with your whole being, in that very seeing is the movement of building anew. The seeing, the listening and the acting are one movement, not separate. To see, to listen, is to free the mind and heart of the past errors, the past mischief, the sorrow that is lying in the mind and heart. To observe so intimately, so closely, is the act of love.

9

YOU HAVE MADE THE MIND
A SLAVE TO WORDS

It was a lovely morning, gentle, soft and full of the morning light. Everything was so very much alive. The birds were singing in the bushes, the trees and in the long hedge. The sun was among the dust-covered leaves and there was that feeling of—if one may use the word—love. The grass, the particle of sand, the feeling that was in you and outside of you were within this sense of extraordinary love. You felt you really loved for the first time and that you never knew it before. It was not emotional sentimentalism or imagination or the excitement that comes with a beautiful morning; it was an incredible feeling that comes unknowingly, without any past memory, with a feeling that every part of you—as the blade of grass and the grain of sand and those birds singing—was of this, indestructible. As you listened to the birds and watched the leaves, everything was in a movement, including yourself, caught up with the vast movement of life which seemed endless and that had no beginning. That morning among the trees, the scented bushes and the dust-coloured leaves there was the feeling of great purity, a world of innocency.

'I have read considerably what you have said about fear. I have tried to understand it as deeply as I could but somehow I am still obsessed by fear. It is not only about little things, superficial affairs, but deep down I have great anxiety, a sense of fear that somehow doesn't seem to go away. I have tried not to name it, to live with it, not to escape from it, as you have said. During many months I have tried to get into touch with it, to be really in communication with it, but yet it doesn't go. So what am I to do?'

What goes wrong with people? Why don't we grow happily, freely, with a great sense of beauty and love? Why doesn't a human being live without any conflict? Why does one allow oneself to be distorted? Why don't we move, live feely without any barrier or resistance, live with a great inward sense of freedom? What goes wrong with us? We are afraid, anxious, worried, confused, weighed down by sorrow, talking about God, doing social work, having beliefs—which all seems so utterly unnecessary. Why do we do all this? What has gone wrong?

The psychologists say it went wrong when your mother fed you on the wrong breast, or the quarrels between your father and mother affected you, or when you were called a sissy on the playing field, or when you gave exaggeration to some particular thing. Surely all these seem so trivial to affect the full flow of life. Are these the real reasons that do affect us, or is there a much deeper, true reason? (Not 'original sin', which Christians trot out when there is no other response to an inquiry.) Why doesn't one grow, live a life that has no conflict, that is not fragmented, that is whole? Is there an answer to this, or no answer at all?

One can give many explanations for why man lives the way he does, but explanations and descriptions are never the described, are never the explained. Explanations do not resolve, clarify and make straight what has been made crooked. You have to look at all this, observe it in yourself, not trying to find an answer but observing it, seeing it and listening to all the mutterings. Then perhaps you will find that you can put away the past. Or rather, the past fades away—the corruption, the conditioning, the crookedness, the distortions. To look, to listen, not for an answer but merely to observe and to listen with all your being, then there is a new movement which is not of the old.

You say, sir, that you have been aware of your fear and of your inquiry into its nature and structure, and yet you are not free of it. Is fear the main issue, or something entirely different?

Is your real problem the question of fear, or is it how to look at the whole movement of life, which includes fear, anxiety, despair, pleasure and the many things that bother us? Can we look at all this as a whole, not as separate things, divided and broken up, look at it all as a free movement, interrelated, not ever separate?

'But I don't know how to look at life that way. I have never looked in this non-dualistic way at life, at myself, or practically at anything, and I don't know how to. I know what you will say if I ask how, that there is no "how", no method, no system. That too I understand because that seems logical and sane. But the fact is I can't look that way.'

Please don't say, 'I can't.' When you use such words you are already creating a barrier. You are falling back into the old habit of saying to yourself that it is not possible or it is possible. One blocks oneself, one prevents oneself from looking. Can you look out of silence? Then this movement is part of the silence. Can you look out of this silence at fear? Not asking what to do with it, or how to suppress or go beyond it, but looking at it out of the depth of silence? To look at the tree, the cloud, your neighbour, at yourself out of this vast silence.

'Again you are asking the impossible of me.'

Sir, we just told you not to use the words impossible or possible, can or cannot. Put those words away from you. Don't be caught by words. Listen to what is being said. Listen with your heart, with your mind, not with the little part of the intellect. Listen to what you have said, that it is not possible. You have hindered yourself by using those words. You have made the mind a slave to the words.

The sun was now getting stronger and the shadows were deepening. The vendor on the road was shouting, calling loud his wares, and a bus went rattling by. The birds were not so noisy; they had withdrawn into the shadows. The day was settling down to the noise, the quarrels, the ambitions, greeds and envies. And the day passes by without ever looking, without ever listening.

10

PLEASURE SOON BECOMES PAIN

The river was golden this morning. The sun was just coming over the treetops and a train was crossing the bridge. The water with that light on it filled your whole horizon. It is the sacred river of India, worshipped by millions and millions of people. It is sacred not only in recent centuries; it always seems to have been worshipped by man. That morning as you watched the light on it you understood why it was sacred. Like all rivers there is something noble, holy about it. This river, which seemed to stretch out to the horizon, was very wide. They say that during the rainy season, the monsoon, it rises over forty feet, practically covering the little village on the other shore. But the waters had subsided and there was a gentle current, but strong in the middle. There was a feeling of great purity, though thousands washed in it, threw their dirt, polluted it in a thousand ways. They threw burned bodies into it, but all that somehow didn't matter. As the sun rose higher the river became molten silver. The light was beginning to be too strong, the sparkles on the water too brilliant, and your eyes couldn't look at it without being disturbed. All day the sun would be blazing hot.

Towards the evening you set out to cross the little stream, with its rickety bridge of mud and bamboo. You went over to the other side, past little villages, mango groves, goats, a herd of cattle, newly planted corn, wheat and peas. This land stretched to the horizon, flat, covered with villages and trees. And poverty was everywhere. The little child would always be hungry and that man sitting on the ground will always have pain. That woman bearing a child will never know the joy of the earth.

Pleasure is one thing and joy is another. Pleasure has motive; joy, ecstasy has none whatever. Pleasure soon becomes pain, involving itself in fear. Pleasure can change from one thing to another; the ending of one pleasure and the seeking of another. Pleasure by itself is very destructive, and when one seeks it one lives in the shadow of fear. Pleasure soon becomes bondage; you are lost without it, you feel empty, you say to yourself, 'What is the purpose, the meaning of life?' And you fill your life with the things of the intellect, from which you derive pleasure. Joy is something entirely different; you can't invite it, it is not at your beck and call. You can't pursue it, you cannot hold it, store it. If you do remember it, it becomes a pleasure and it is no longer joy.

Pleasure, with all its values and moralities, its fears and ambitions, its competitive drive, with its experiences, knowledge and remembrances, is the 'me', the ego, the 'I'. In pleasure there is always a division between the 'me' and the thing from which the 'me' derives pleasure. The seeker of the pleasure and the thing from which one derives pleasure are two separate things, in conflict with each other. Where there is separation there must be conflict; that is inevitable. Joy is not yours. You cannot cultivate it, whereas you can cultivate pleasure. You cannot run after joy; it is there when you are not there. You and joy cannot exist together. In joy there is no separation. Ecstasy is not exclusive; in it there are no fragmentations as the 'you' and 'me', 'we' and 'they'. Pleasure can never become joy. There is no road leading from one to the other. The mind that seeks pleasure cannot come to joy, but when there is joy then pleasure has quite a different meaning.

The path led through filthy villages; people sitting in the dust of a thousand years. Goats nibbled at branches and leaves that had been cut down from the trees that lined the pathway. Those trees would die soon for they are being stripped daily of their precious leaves. But the villager doesn't care; what he is concerned with is to feed the goats. A little further on there was a deep well and a woman singing was drawing water from it. She was poor, dirty, never knowing the beauty that surrounded her, the richness of the earth and the light on the leaves. She never looked around, she hadn't the energy. She just had enough to draw the water and cook a meal over a little fire, hungry from morning to night, until she dies.

Nobody seems to care. Many explanations are given for why these villagers are like that, why people are what they are—the climate, the lack of food, the overpopulation. There are many peripheral explanations, but passion has gone out of life. The passion that cares, that works, that gives, that creates, simply is not there. Governments squabble over their theories, their particular systems, and the woman is forgotten. She will live and die in poverty, in squalor, ignorant, diseased, for she has no hope anymore. There is only the dark despair and the flash of the sunlight on the water.

11

COMPARISON BREEDS DISCONTENT

Four vultures were sitting on the tall tamarind, bare-necked, huge birds with enormous wings. They looked at the river, waiting for carcasses to float by—human carcasses as well as dead animals. Two or three vultures would land on them and keep the crows away. They would have their fill and come back to a tree. But this morning they were sitting very peacefully, motionless. Presently five crows came and began to tease the vultures, going up to them, pulling their wings or flapping their own wings against them, until one of them flew off and a crow would try to ride on its back. They kept this up for at least half an hour until the vultures went off across the river. The crows came back, enjoying themselves hugely, calling to each other.

It was a fresh, clear morning full of light. The waters of the river were alive with a quality that seemed to hold the entire light of the universe. This morning they were especially without a movement; there wasn't a single ripple, very quiet, motionless. As the sun rose over the trees on the other bank, the river became golden and presently turned into silver. The beauty and love of the earth were immense.

We crossed the rickety bridge over the shallow, dirty stream, went up the bank and along the sacred way of pilgrims for thousands of years, towards the place where the Buddha preached. There were tamarinds, mangos, little villages and empty shrines.

'I am so discontented. I have a little money, I don't have to go to an office day after day and waste my life, but I'm eaten up with discontent. I read, I meditate, I talk to people, which delights me, but soon this discontent, this deep restlessness comes over me and no book, no meditation, nothing seems to bring quiet. Presently this discontent fades away and I'm back with my eagerness for meditation, groping after my own depths, inquiring into my mind, asking, questioning, looking. Pretty soon, without my wanting it, this discontent, this restlessness comes like a wave over me, almost smothers me. For several years I have heard what you have been saying. I have attended many of your talks, discussed with others, but somehow after these years the burden of discontent, the restlessness, remains with me. I don't know what to do.'

Another said, 'I have lived here for two years. I have been all over, seen many of the beautiful things of this country, the dances, the marvellous colours, the beautiful land, the hills, the mountains and the rivers. Naturally, I have talked with many of the people, but through it all I feel this country is falling apart, breaking down, disintegrating. I am not trying to compare this country with other countries; I am looking at it, as you have often pointed out, with eyes that do not condemn, that do not have prejudices or fanciful conclusions. But there is, I feel, a great decline. Probably it has always been that way, before the British and after them, and I wonder what is going to happen.

'Of course, the politicians are never going to solve the problems, nor the sannyasis, nor the pundits. Just look at that woman now, how ill she looks, dirty, without a spark of energy. The child she is carrying is so small, so full of tears, and rarely ever laughter. Disease, poverty and its degradation is all over the land. I don't know what to do. There are so many millions like this. Neither the government nor the people seem to care; everybody has become so callous, indifferent. And I often watch it and have tears in my heart and my eyes. I am not depressed or looking with despair, but I often wonder what's going to happen. I suppose a few want power, like others right through the world. Like all the politicians of the world, with their jargon and exclusive parties, with their ideologies, chicanery and hypocrisy, they promise so much but their promises are empty words.

'Living here, I help a little, each person as much as I can, but I know too that doesn't solve anything. It is like a vast river full of volume, of great depth, moving towards the sea. This country is like that, but the land, the hills, the rice fields, the snow-covered mountains are something extraordinarily beautiful. Perhaps they will bring some contentment to this hungry land.'

Another one said, 'I too find myself not wanting to do anything. I have to earn a livelihood but I don't want to do anything. I am frightened to spend the rest of my days typing or taking down shorthand, or manipulating a machine, or teaching in a school. I am really frightened of doing any of these things. My money won't last me perhaps more than a year and after that I have to work. I don't want to take the responsibility of working. I don't want to be responsible to anything or to anybody. I have worked but I find it bores me. At the end of two months I got so frightened I left everything.'

The sun was setting among clouds and the sky was golden, violet, and parts of it were green, that subtle, pale yellow green. The beauty of the earth stretched before you, field after field, tree after tree, and in the distance were the mountains.

Why are you discontented? What is the meaning of this restlessness? Is it that you want your mind to be occupied with something and therefore it is searching, looking for something that will interest it? Is it that it wants complete and total absorption in some action, wants to commit itself to something, to a belief, to an activity? Is that the reason why it is so restless? Is there something that you are deeply, vitally interested in, so that the interest absorbs this restlessness and discontent?

'I don't think I am particularly interested in anything. I worked but nothing seems to interest me. I soon get tired of it, bored. I want to leave everything and go away. And when I do go away, I'm again restless after a while. And this flame of discontent burns, reaching a point of despair. I read and escape but I am soon back again.'

Has this discontent come about because you live in a world of comparison, comparing yourself with another, thinking in terms of more, saying this is better than that? Are you caught in the words more, better, and so on? Is comparison bringing about this discontent or are you trying to find a means of smothering this discontent?

'I am not trying to suppress it or put a cover on it; I am trying to live with it, understand it, find out why it exists. But I haven't been able to. Perhaps the real reason, as you point out, is that I am comparing myself with somebody else.'

This conditioning that is brought about through comparison begins from childhood, in the school, in the college, in the university, and up and up, always comparing oneself with another, with the superior technocrat, with the saint, with the rich man or with the man who is in power. Or you are comparing yourself with an ideal or an image which you yourself have put together. This constant comparison must breed discontent.

'Yes, I have been comparing myself with you. I see now that that too must go away, the image I have built about you with which I have been comparing. Then I can be myself.'

The 'yourself' is the result of this comparison. You are the comparative mind; and when you say, 'When I don't compare I'll be myself,' what you will be is still the result of the conditioning of comparison. There can be no being yourself. Yourself is the result of the process of time, of comparison, of despair and sorrow, pleasure and fear. So what matters is not to be yourself but to live without comparison. When you do that your mind has a different quality, it lives at a different dimension. Then you have enormous energy. The burden of the comparative spirit is put away; you are lighter, freer.

Ah! I am using the words lighter, freer—*that again is comparison; we don't mean that. You are light, your whole being is free from the burden which has been accumulated for centuries. Can you live one day without ever comparing yourself with another, to have the non-comparative mind, a mind that observes without comparison, without measurement? For there is great illusion in measurement, in the mind that says, 'I have been, and I will be something more.' This measurement leads to every form of deception, hypocrisy and strife. When the mind is completely free of all comparison there is real freedom.*

'Yes, I see that. I am already feeling lighter. I see where I have taken the wrong turn—again "lighter", "wrong". I don't mean wrong in the moral sense. I see where I have been caught. I never thought about this and I am beginning to see wide space and great release of energy.'

12

WHAT BRINGS ABOUT PERCEPTION?

The action of thought is one thing and the action of perception is another. The action of thought must inevitably lead to confusion and to bondage. It has a quality of time-binding, whereas seeing and doing is a movement in freedom. One is a form of resistance in continuity, the other is the total absence of any form of resistance, defence or aggressive pursuit. Thought sees that demanding a particular attitude destroys relationship, and comes to a conclusion or a decision that it must not pursue that path. But in the very decision is its continuity.

Thought can analyse the destructive nature of possessing in relationship and push away from itself, underground into the unconscious, the idea that it must not pursue a particular desire. But it remains there; thought has only pushed it further away from itself. In this analytical process, thought doesn't bring about right relationship. It is still the action of thought considering itself to be love. The other, the seeing and the doing, is entirely different. In seeing and doing there is no implication or analysis of thought whatsoever.

Thought cannot perceive in the total sense of that word. Analysis cannot bring about perception. Then what does bring about perception? Does thought bring it about, or the absence of thought? If perception is something that has come about through the medium of thought then it is still not the freedom of perception—acting then is according to a pattern set by thought in the present or the past. Therefore that action is incomplete and not free.

How does perception come without the interference

of thought? What is the nature of perception? What is the structure? What makes the mind, including the heart, see something so clearly that the very seeing is the acting? Does analysis bring this about? Or is it that after analysing and the exhaustion brought about through analysis, the mind becomes quiet and perception takes place? That implies that analysis is a primary requisite—but is it? Or is all analysis futile? In analysis there is always the analyser and the analysed, and therefore there is duality, conflict and decision, which really is a form of resistance. If this is understood, it is very clear that analysis has no place in perception. Seeing, doing, takes place instantly but in analysis there is always a remnant of the past. When a decision is made according to the past it is still within the field of time and therefore idea and action are two separate states, two separate activities, hence duality, conflict and contradiction.

How does perception and immediate action happen? Does it depend on the sensitivity of the mind, the heart, the brain, the nerves, so intelligence is awake, working, and when there is any form of crisis or challenge it responds immediately and acts? If it is the result of previous perceptions or actions, it is memory that responds and action then is still the old, still the product of thought.

So perception is really the quality of the mind that has become highly sensitive and therefore intelligent. This intelligence operates when any danger is seen—the danger of nationalism, of postponement, of the interference of thought. There is grave danger in all that. So, being sensitive and therefore intelligent, it is this intelligence that sees and acts, and not thought at all.

Intelligence is not the product of thought, because thought is memory, the response of experience, tradition, knowledge, and that cannot possibly bring about intelligence. Intelligence is freedom to act; to act in a totally different dimension at a totally different level. The past, which is thought, has no place and cannot bring about intelligence.

How does intelligence come about? The mind with its brain cells—and *mind* also means the heart—sees the full implication of thought because it has seen the danger of analysis and its dualistic state as the analyser and the analysed. The sensitivity of the mind sees that because it has observed, it has looked; therefore the sensitivity has come about without thought. It is this quality of sensitivity that perceives and acts instantly.

This is what we do when we meet great danger, physical danger. It is like meeting a snake; there is instant response. That response is the conditioned response, conditioned for millions of years to protect from danger. That protection is essential and that protection is the action of intelligence, not of fear. Intelligence has discovered that to survive you must run away from snakes. Fear only resists or gets excited, does some foolish thing. With intelligence, when there is danger there is instant action. That same intelligence operates when there is psychological danger if the mind is extraordinarily awake. When there is psychological danger to a mind that is awake and alert, a mind that has been watching, there is instant action. In this there is no duality, it is a surgical operation, and therefore no conflict, no residue as resistance or thought.

13

CAN MY CHILD'S BRAIN CELLS BE CHANGED?

She was a young mother, full of a great deal of affection, care and concern for her son. She seemed so nice, pleasant, with her long black hair, highly polished in the light. She sat down on the floor as the others were also doing and began to talk about her young child.

One could hear the noises of the street, the vendor, the children playing, the car struggling up the hill and someone calling aloud. And beyond all this noise was the sea. It wasn't blue, it was rather dull, grey and muddy. It was a warm morning and it was winter.

She said, 'My son, five and a half years old, is terribly selfish. Anything around him he wants, clings to and fights for. When anyone takes anything away from him, he cries and insists on having his own way. I have talked to him as much as one can talk to a young child of that age. I have scolded him. Often I am tempted to beat him but I have resisted. And this grabbing, this wanting everything for himself, this deep selfishness seems to be increasing. At a party with other children he fights. Other children cry, resist, and somehow through wheedling, through anger, he gets his own way. He gets what he wants at the end of it, at least from all the children of his own age. I don't know quite what to do.

'I heard you last night and one of the things you said struck me. You said, if I remember rightly, that the very brain structure itself must undergo a mutation. I lay awake half the night thinking about it and considered my child, how to bring about that mutation in the brain so that he can be unselfish, grow into a decent human being, with affection, care, and appreciate the beauty of life and all the goodness of the earth, instead of wanting everything for himself and building a wall around himself. So I thought I would come along this morning with the others to talk over this mutation of the brain cells. May I ask, can my son's brain cells be changed so that he is not selfish anymore, so that he can live a happy life, instead of always wanting, wanting, grabbing, fighting, with violence and the rest of the misery of life?'

The vendor was shouting in a loud voice, asking for old newspapers, and his cry came into the room. A man was playing a flute. He had begun that morning very early, before four o'clock. He was practising then, and now he was walking along the road with so many shadows in the brilliant sunshine, playing his little tune.

Don't you think the first thing is to observe? Observe the ways of his selfishness, of his violence, the subtleties he uses to get what he wants. Then after having observed, see that you as the mother have completely put aside the desire to change the boy, and have no desire of any kind to bring about a mutation, a wiping away of this selfish pursuit. Never compare him with somebody who is less selfish. Never punish or reward him. If you do, you have the instinctual desire to change him according to your own pattern of what life or the boy should be, or the pattern which society or some ideal has set. That is why it is very important to wipe away from your heart and mind this desire to change him. Also see that any form of punishment and reward is still within the field of the desire to bring about a change. Then see that you don't yourself set an example for him. If you do, because you give him comfort, a feeling of security, he might change, but that change will again transform itself into selfishness. Through imitation, through conformity, the brain cells cannot be altered. Nor can there be a mutation in the brain cells themselves if you set him an example or point out how other boys are unselfish, how good they are, how pleasant to live with and so on. All that implies the deep desire on your part to change him. And this desire, though it may not be expressed, is consciously or unconsciously influencing him and therefore making him more uncertain, insecure. And this insecurity, this uncertainty makes him feel more, makes him ask for more, defend himself, resist, become more selfish.

So you, the mother who is watching the boy, must wipe away from your mind and heart any desire for change, that he should become something which he is not through example, through punishment, through reward, through an ideal and so on. Because this creates in him a sense of insecurity, and it is this very insecurity, probably, that is making him so self-centred, so selfish.

'Then what *is* one to do? If I am not to correct him, if I'm not to tell him or to control or punish him or do all the things that you have said, what is left? How can I deal with the boy?'

How do you deal with the boy when he cries his heart out over some silly thing, sobbing, shouting, agonising? Don't you put him in your lap, hug him, caress him, talk to him gently, make him feel that he can turn to you or you are his security, you're his mother who understands, who loves? Do you see what we mean?

What is the state of your mind, your heart, when you have wiped away all these things, these condemnations, justifications, evaluations and formulas? What is the feeling, the quality that is in your mind and heart? Isn't there the sense of love? When it is there you then hug him, put him in your lap, talk to him gently, not in terms of reward and punishment; you talk to him about the sunset, this or that, make him feel completely secure. Because there is love he will feel the freedom of it. Condemnation does not enter at all into love. It is this love that is going to bring about a mutation in the brain cells themselves. It acts as a shock—if one may use that word shock *with love. Perhaps then the brain cells themselves undergo a change without any pressure, without any effort, without obedience and authority. It is like being exposed to the bright sun. Resistance and isolation are a form of insecurity and therefore they breed conflict; and that expresses itself in selfish activity—as in the case of the child grabbing things, crying when he can't get something. Any form of subtle threat or reward breeds a sense of insecurity. When that is not there love does have an effect. When the mind and heart are completely free of every condemnation or justification there is the feeling of utter security both psychologically and physically. That doesn't mean that one builds a wall of resistance round oneself or withdraws into isolation. Love is a tremendous thing, and* that *acts. That is the only action that can possibly bring about a mutation in the brain cells.*

14

CHOICE EXISTS ONLY WHEN THE MIND IS CONFUSED

The smell of rain was on the land. It had been a good monsoon and the trees and the green rice fields were full of life. There had not been such a good monsoon as this for several years and you could feel the rejoicing of the land as you entered into the valley. The valley was remote, unspoilt, not crowded with exploding population. The villagers were still villagers, poor, cheerful, uncomplaining, dancing when the festivities demanded. They worked all day and at night. They drank a little too; with several good drinks they were ready for dance and folklore, with drums, pipes and cymbals. The rain had filled the wells and the lake, and the dams were now holding the water. You really could feel the joy of the earth. Every shining leaf told the tale as the light of the morning sun shone upon them. There was all the light of the earth and at night the light of the moon. And there was the light of your own heart if you gave your heart to it. As you sat on the platform you saw in the distance through a gap between trees a sculptured hill with a solitary rock standing on the top of it, as though very carefully put there by great machinery and great labour of man. It must have been there for many, many, many centuries. They say that these hills are the oldest hills in the world and, strangely, they have the shapes of temples, peculiar shapes as though very carefully put together by a great architect. You saw the beauty of the land, the sweep of those hills and the green fields going up to the foot of them. The red earth that was very old held a great silence.

It was a morning of great delight and great beauty.

Choice exists only when the mind is confused

Tamarind, the palm tree and the mango seemed to fill the valley and every leaf was sparkling. Bougainvillea, the rose and the many thousand little flowers were exploding with colour. You could hardly take your eyes from them. Their welcoming beauty filled your eyes and you saw nothing and heard nothing but what they had to say. It was really a most marvellous morning of purity, of great silence and tranquillity. You hardly dared to move, let alone talk to the great throng of people waiting.

Earlier that morning as you looked out of the window you saw monkeys, the small ones with red faces and yellowish-brown hair. They were very destructive. They came in bands, picked up what they could and left. Small babies with white bellies were no longer clinging to their mothers but were jumping from branch to branch restlessly. They made almost human gestures. There were two of them sitting very close together watching the man behind the window. They were very still, as was the man. If he made the slightest move they would run away, and yet they were within arm's reach. They seemed unafraid, terribly curious.

Higher up the tree on a branch was what must have been their mother, watching. And the whole valley, the hills and the marvellous old trees were all waiting, watching. 'I seem to have spent my life choosing between what is right, what should be, what I must do and must not do. It has been a great struggle to choose always the right thing. There are desires and appetites, old memories and deep-rooted inclinations to fight off. As long as I can remember, I seem to be always choosing. Not only the clothes I put on and their colour but also choosing between right and wrong, about going to the office, between action and inaction, between laziness and activity, between the dreary life and pleasant solitude.

'When I am driving I catch myself choosing whether I should take this road or that road, though I know both roads very well. I am always weighing between this and that. I think most of us do this, though perhaps with some it is a conscious, deliberate choice and with others it is unconscious movement. But this movement of division is always there with all of us. It is an endless corridor of opposites and I seem to be moving from one thing to another all the time.

'The other day, by chance, I came to one of your talks and you said something about choice being a waste of energy, leading to greater confusion and conflict. You said definitely that choice is conflict. Did you say it to provoke thought or state it as a matter of truth? I would like to talk about this with you if I may. Why are you so much against choice?

'Freedom implies choice. Freedom to choose is man's great hope. If I cannot choose I have no freedom. If I cannot choose between this job and that job, or to go from this town to that town, and am always restricted by government or by law, then freedom comes to an end. If I cannot choose between this belief and that, I am not a free agent, or if I cannot choose a political or a religious person as leader.

'So when I consider it, choice seems to be one of the great assets that human beings have cultivated throughout the ages. But you say choice is the very denial of freedom. I am not one who will accept easily what another says. I have to choose what seems to me reasonable and have the feeling that it is true, not have the stupid acceptance of a follower.'

If you see very clearly, what is the need of choice? Choice exists only when the mind is confused. The fact is that being uncertain, confused and therefore not able to see clearly, out of this, choice is made. You choose your leader according to your prejudice, your confusion, political or otherwise. You choose according to your temperament, to your peculiar idiosyncrasies and taste. Your taste, your idiosyncrasy and tendency is the cause of confusion. You have your confusion and the other has his. He chooses his leader and you choose whom you shall follow, and so there is a division between your truth and his truth, between your leader and his leader. And where there is division there is conflict.

Conflict's very nature and structure is confusion. We say, 'That is my characteristic, my character,' and give great importance to character, to your quality, your peculiar behaviour, your peculiar twist of thought and feeling. This you call your individuality. That individuality is broken up into fragments. These many fragments, conscious or unconscious, are what you call the characteristics of an individual. But the very word individual *means indivisible, not fragmented and therefore not confused. When an individual is broken up, as he is, and therefore he is not an individual, these many fragments are in opposition to each other and in their contradiction bring about confusion.*

Out of this confusion you choose, so your leader, your beliefs and prejudices must also be confused. You choose out of confusion. What is important is not choice but the clearing up of confusion, or rather the ending of confusion so that there is clear perception. So perception is what matters and not choice. When there is clear perception there is no need for choice at all. Choice demands resistance, assertion of will and a subtle process of isolation, which puts an end to all relationship and to love.

So exploration is not in the field of choice but into the field of seeing, hearing and learning—which are really one. It is to see without any distortion, without any fragmentation, to see wholly, with sanity, with what that word whole *implies, which is holy. It is to see the truth of this, not according to your truth or to your peculiarities or my peculiarities but to see without any distortion. This puts an end to all choice and therefore to all effort. A protestant, a communist or a Hindu and so on, is not able to see things as they are, wholly, because he is conditioned. It is this conditioning that is called character, which is a form of resistance cultivated in a particular culture or social structure.*

So to live without any choice is true freedom. It is not within the borders of a particular culture and doesn't create its own borders. It moves without building the banks which hold the movement. After all, love is that. In love there is no choice or effort or contradiction. When love is translated as pleasure, desire and the pursuit of an enjoyable memory, then that brings about the narrow banks within which the small stream flows, with the noise of despair and agony.

'All criticism is impossible. What you say seems to be so absolutely right. It comes down to a very simple fact: either I see or I don't see. If I don't see, I am confused, blinded by my sorrow.'

15

CONTROL IN ANY FORM IS DISTORTION

That morning the river was flowing silver. From ice melted in the mountains it went down through the plains towards the sea. As it was a slightly misty morning, the golden light of the sun as it came up over the trees made the water red and gold. It was a magnificent river, wide and deep. It was a sacred river but the beauty of it was not that it was sacred, but that such a stretch of water gave to the land a sense of peace, strength and vitality. In the evening it was different; the sun behind the big city made it golden again but entirely different from what it was in the morning. It was always changing, its mood was never the same. You looked at it ten times a day and each hour brought something new to it. On each bank it was sullied with filth and you didn't want to touch it, but midstream the blue waters were surprisingly clean where there was a strong current. You wanted to touch it, to drink it, to swim in it. That morning, with the light of the rising sun, the sparkling waters brought to the mind the peace that lay on the land.

The sun was getting warm and we withdrew into the darker room and sat quietly on the floor, looking at the tamarind and the blue sky and listening to some voices in the far distance. He seemed quite contented to talk about himself and wasn't at all embarrassed to talk about his problems to a complete stranger. He was a big man, well fed. He had difficulty in sitting down on the floor but he managed it, and once he settled down he never moved.

'I was very surprised', he said, 'the other morning to hear you ask why one should control oneself at all. You said,

"Why have discipline; what is the need for conformity and adjustment?" It gave me rather a shock when I heard you. You explained it very carefully but I couldn't get beyond the words. I have always controlled myself, in various ways, and to suddenly be told that control or self-imposed discipline is a waste of energy, a form of stupid satisfaction, was a bit upsetting.

'I think I am modern in my outlook on life. I've been abroad, seen the modern movement, the revolt of the young, the peculiarities of that generation who think they are quite different from the older generation. But they are even more conformist; they look almost like each other, dress alike, and it is hard to distinguish between a boy and a girl. Yet they are constantly asserting that they are in revolt. I don't think I am modern in that way. The young complain against the old and the old condemn the behaviour of the young. This has been going on for many thousand years. Socrates, too, complained.

'I went to university and got a degree. I was enthusiastic and idealistic to see things changed, not only at the political level but a change in society. I have been through youthful experiments in communism and I am in revolt, not only against the culture in which I have been brought up but also in revolt in myself.

'In your talk you were more revolutionary than the extreme left or right. It gave me quite a jolt. Were you really serious when you said that control in any form is distortion, and that action born out of that must inevitably create disharmony and misery? It is so surprising I can't believe my own ears. Am I to set aside all my controls, all my willpower, all the ways which I have set myself to follow? I would be completely lost. I would be in disorder. What keeps me in order is the sense of control, direction, restraint. I hope you understand what my difficulty is.'

You are saying that without direction and control you

would be lost; life would be disordered and society would go to pieces. Let's explore together this complicated issue of freedom and control. We talk about control. Obviously in it there is the controller and the controlled. The controller has gathered knowledge through experience and tradition. He is aware that if he does not think, act, function according to past information, there would be greater conflict in meeting the present. So he becomes convinced that control is supreme, all-important. He does not see the division that has taken place between himself and the thing to be controlled, shaped or directed. He is separate and his desires, appetite and urges are something apart over which he must have control. He is the censor with a whip in his hand. When there is such division, conflict naturally comes about—one must dominate the other.

'Yes, I see that is a fact. I am different from the impulse, the desire, the lust. I cannot control my biting appetites that lead me and therefore there is fear, for God knows where they would lead me.'

And so fear demands control; fear of what might happen. The controller has the aching memory of what he thinks should be. In that, again there is division and the continuance of fear. So we are asking why there should be a controller at all, or resistance, or a goal. Control implies not only the division between the one who controls and that which is to be controlled, but there is also suppression with its empty frustrations, neurotic thoughts and activity. If you don't do that, you try to sublimate, escape. The object of your escapes becomes far more important than the resolution.

The implied question is why there is division at all.

Control means division. Division is not only at the peripheral level of one's existence but also at the very core of one's being, at the very root of one's action. Division implies the 'me' and the 'not me'. The 'me' is always trying to control, dominate; and the 'not me' must fit into the mould of 'me'. This is the battle between human beings, nation against nation and so on. We accept this division as a natural human characteristic—the Supreme and the human.

When you see the truth of what this division implies—the truth, not the intellectual concept of the truth—when you see this, actually taste it, feel it, not as an opinion or agreement or judgement, which depends on environmental influence and so on, this truth, the absolute fact of it, makes the mind shed the controller, put away his concepts of what should be, so there is only what is *and not how to control it. A mind that is free of the censor no longer has any problem with* what is. *It tells its own story, and the listening to the story is the action of that story. So action comes in the act of listening, not in the action of the censor or the controller.*

The activity of the censor or the controller becomes empty and futile, but the action of listening to the story of what is *is the love of doing, without reward or punishment. The controller always has a motive; in listening to* what is *there is no motive. When there is no motive there is the action of love. If you control love then it is pleasure with all its agony. So love is not a thing to be chastened or controlled by thought with its controls, sanctions and directives that make love empty, without significance.*

16

SOLITUDE MEANS FREEDOM

We had been up there for several weeks. The cabin was crude, rough; the windows had no panes and rats and birds came in and out. In a week's time the bulbul were eating out of your hand. They loved raisins more than anything else and it was a delight to see them enjoy themselves. They would eat practically all day long if you fed them. And the rats stole your letters. Tucked away in a hole, the blue paper just showing, we found a letter which was not answered. Luckily they hadn't eaten it or pulled it down any further and we were able to pull it out and answer it.

It had been warm, almost hot, at that altitude. Clouds gathered and it was a marvellous sight to see those immense, dark, threatening clouds full of rain. It rained day after day and the smell of the earth was fresh, fragrant and full of joy. Now the sky was blue, rain-washed, and the mountains which had been hidden for nearly ten days were now visible. Some of the peaks were twenty-five thousand feet. They were full of fresh snow, glistening in the morning light. A valley lay below, dark, deep, filled with a blue vapour. You could see, they said, three hundred miles of snow peaks. It really was a marvellous sight that morning. It was quite breathless and now the ten days of rain had made the earth green, washed the dust of the summer off the leaves. There were fresh leaves on practically every tree, on every bush, and every blade of grass was bold and crisp.

Presently, into the cabin came six monks, freshly washed. Their saffron-coloured robes had been washed, too, that morning. We sat on the floor. They sat with their backs to the view and probably never saw the glory and the beauty of those mountains, which were something incredible to see and to feel with their solitude and distance. The monks were rather intellectual and therefore rather emotional.

Probably most intellectuals are rather emotional and that is why they get caught so easily in theories, utopias and ideological fancies. There they were, with clean faces; some of them were rather fat and others were lean, sharp-eyed. They seemed to have extraordinary vitality for they had been on a journey high up in the mountains to see their guru who they said lived alone and was very wise. Solitude and wisdom seemed to live up there. They had been climbing for days, travelling from the south to the north, and now they thought they would like to come and pay respect, as they called it.

Is the guru really in solitude or is he full of knowledge, full of the tradition and wisdom of others? When asked that question they all seemed so very surprised. One of them said, 'We had never thought that solitude was something that could be free from knowledge and tradition, from the Vedas and the Upanishads.'

If you carry the Vedas and the Upanishads and all the teachings in your mind, then you really are never in solitude, are you? You are always living with others and through others. Solitude means freedom, freedom to be completely alone, unburdened by the past, without the future across the abyss or beyond those lovely mountains.

The monks seemed utterly bewildered for they had gone up to see the guru to bring back his wisdom and give to other people what they had learned, teach them the wisdom they carried. And now there they were, sitting solemnly with a surprised look, for they could not see that freedom and solitude means the state of aloneness where the mind is totally innocent, incapable of being hurt with knowledge. The more one talked to them, the more they became bewildered, unhappy and uncertain, for their pilgrimage meant so much to them, and what was being said was destroying everything that they had built around themselves, in themselves. They were an unhappy lot as they left but you could see as they went down the hill in their brightly coloured robes that the past was overtaking them. What we said was merely incidental, something to be left behind as though it may have some truth in it but it wasn't for them.

They went down the steep path past the green meadows, crossing a little bridge over a torrent, and they disappeared round a bend. You knew in your heart that they would never come near you again, for it was too much. But the mountains and the deep valley and the green meadow and the torrent understood what it meant to be completely alone, untouched by all the things that man has put together—character, virtue, action and God.

17

CAN THE MIND UNBURDEN ITSELF?

A small group came to the cabin. They asked for blessing and sat on the ground on the rough mat, not looking at the marvellous trees in bloom, the butterflies, the mynah birds and the bulbul that sat on a branch singing. It was a lovely morning, full of delicate sunshine; the air had a perfume of the mountains, the pines and the smell of rich earth.

One of them said, 'One must take a long journey, perhaps through many lives. At least in this life, the journey is very long. You go through so many things, so many experiences, so many events that you are burdened with them all. It is not like a mountaineer who climbs with hardly anything. But we are not mountaineers, we are human beings and we carry from day to day, year after year, all the burdens, not only of our forefathers but our own, the traditions, the habits, the multiplying sorrows. We plod heavily through and we think we are moving forward. I know in my heart, not only with my reason and logic, that these burdens must be set aside to travel lightly, freely. But there they are. What I really want to ask is if these burdens must be removed one by one or is there a total unburdening at one given moment and being completely free? I don't know if I am making my question clear.'

I think it is fairly clear. You are saying, aren't you sir, that the burdens, as you call them, are the things that you have accumulated, the many, many layers which man has put on himself, round himself, in himself. And you are asking whether they should be peeled off bit by bit, chiselled away, or if the whole of that can be set aside on the instant, so one moves forward without the slightest weight, the slightest hindrance of the past.

'I have seen the futility of endlessly trying to examine things, of trying to peel off different problems one by one as they come up, but what has been difficult is to try either to find the root, the key source of problems and to go to that, past all its manifestations, or to try to see a total something that is the problem, so that nothing is left out of that. And somewhere I fall rather hopelessly between these two efforts and I am unable to find either.'

Is it really a problem? Is it a question of moving or putting away or analysing one issue after another? Or is it something entirely different that you are trying to ask? You must have seen for yourself quite clearly that the analytical process does not lead anywhere.

'It seems to be a string of beads, one bead leading to another bead, and there is no end to this process. But one hopes to come to, as it were, a root bead, a single bead from which others derive.'

But if it is the single bead attached to other smaller beads through a string, it is still part of the rosary.

'I suppose I hope to find a central significance in what we have just called the root bead, and by understanding that single all-important bead the rest will dissolve. But this seems a most imperfect procedure, or perhaps an impossible one. Could you speak more about seeing the whole of something? This is something, to my mind, so enormous that one doesn't know what to do in front of such an effort. When does one know that one has seen the whole? We don't know the dimensions of the whole.'

Sir, I wonder if that is really the question—seeing the whole, peeling off layer after layer, the analytical process, the time element in all this.

'But are you not suggesting that in seeing the whole there is no time element or peeling off; that that perception of a whole is the thing itself? When one considers such a thing, not having done it, it is bewildering. It is hard to know what a whole really is in this life. What do you mean by the whole of something? May one ask that?'

You started out wanting to take a journey and knowing that to take a really long journey you must travel lightly. You said that you are carrying a great weight. The question really is, is it not—I'm just asking, I'm not imposing a question on you—whether this burden can be totally set aside? It is not the perception of the whole that will help you to set the burden aside, but the quality of the mind that is capable of it or that happily and easily puts this weight away from itself.

'Are you saying that it is not the right question to ask what the action is, but rather what the state of the mind is which will act and not ask a question?'

Yes, not what the action is but rather what the quality of the mind is that acts. I think the two are entirely different.

'Well, may one then ask what you mean by a state of mind?'

I wouldn't even use that word state.

'Or quality; you have said quality.'

I think quality, because it is a living thing—a state is more or less static.

'But you have in a sense ruled out an inquiry about action. Therefore we are now trying to look at a quality.'

Yes, because action will take place when we have understood the quality of the mind.

'So for the moment, for the purposes of this inquiry, we put aside any questions about what the action might be. Is that correct, for the moment, just for the moment?'

No, it is not for the moment—*I wouldn't put it that way. You can't set action aside, because life* is *action, every moment is action. The mind is more important than the action which springs from the quality of the mind. So we must think together of the quality of the mind which can put the oldest burden aside. The putting aside is the action of that quality of the mind.*

'Sir, how does one go about this, where do we start?'

That is the whole point. It is not where do we start. That is a dangerous question to ask because then where is the beginning and where is the end? If we say there is a beginning and there is an end, there is a distance, a time, an interval, a journeying between the beginning and the end; whereas the beginning is the end, the means is the end.

'Yes. Yes, I see that. And yet where are we?'

Where are we? I can't help asking you to look at those mountains. Do turn and look! See the fresh snow and the dark valley below and those birds on the tree and the flowering bushes. See all that! Now, when you see all that, what relationship has that seeing to the burden which you carry?

'When I look at the mountain and the birds, the burden is gone and for the moment I have no interest or thought of it. But when I turn away from the mountain the burden is there again.'

When you looked at those mountains they had really no relationship to you. You were looking at them as an observer who is objectively or emotionally looking at something which has nothing to do with your daily life. But these burdens are part of you, part of your life, part of your everyday movement. And we ask, what is the relationship between the seeing of those mountains and the burden which you carry? How do you look at those burdens? You look as a man who wants to get rid of them, as a man who feels that they are unbearable, that you ought to suppress them, destroy them, put them away. So in your observation of your burden there is resistance in your eye, there is condemnation. Resistance and condemnation don't exist when you look at those mountains.

'When I look at the mountains there is delight; when I look at the burden there is pain.'

Obviously.

'From my point of view, is it such a different looking?'

When you look at the burden, aren't you looking with the eyes of experience, with the eyes that have knowledge about the burden?

'But the burden is experience. There is no objective burden that my eyes see, as there is when I look at a mountain. There is a something in myself causing pain, which I described as a burden. It is presumably knowledge and experience that has created it. But for me it is as real as the mountain.'

Sir, you are really asking a very simple question; let's not make it terribly complicated. You are asking if you can put away these burdens happily and freely, immediately, and not go through the process of investigation, analysis and all the rest of it. Is that the question?

'Yes.'

If that is the question, and if you are really serious about it—and I presume you are because you have taken a lot of trouble to come up here—you are asking if this is possible. No, the word possible *is not it. Can this happen without all the struggle against it, without all the effort involved in it? Can it naturally, freely happen that this burden falls away? One should never ask for a method—never! Because method again implies a burden. When you want to get rid of a great many burdens through a method, that very method becomes a burden. That is fairly clear. Therefore never ask of anybody a method, a system of freeing the mind from its self-created burdens.*

If this is really clear then what is the quality of your mind now which faces a problem without having a method, without asking itself what to do with it? Is the mind free from time, analysis, resistance, a direction towards which it is trying to go, or from saying the burdens must go?

'But sir, if the mind were that way there would be no burden and therefore...'

Therefore that is the only question, not the burden.

'Can the burdened mind ask that question?'

It is asking now. Can the mind, which is already burdened so heavily, conditioned through centuries, unburden itself? That is what you are asking, aren't you?

'That is what I have asked, yes. But unless I misunderstand, you are asking if the mind can ask without any of that.'

Yes, because if it asks with all that, then there is no answer. Then the mind is caught in a trap and says it can't get out of a trap.

'But sir, it is as though you are saying that you must get out of the trap in order to ask the question that will get you out of the trap. This becomes a conundrum, a bewildering situation for the mind that is in the trap.'

No, first of all we are saying: what is the quality of the mind that looks at the burden? That is all we are asking; the quality, the nature of the mind that looks at the burden which it has created. If the quality of that mind is still thinking of how to get rid of the burden, how to put it away from itself, that implies resistance, time and analysis. If the mind sees that it is a false approach—sees it not verbally but actually sees it, tastes it, smells it—then does the burden exist at all?

'Are you saying that you must cease to identify yourself with the burden?'

No, we are not saying that you must put an end to identification with the burden.

'I am tempted to say that what you are saying is you must be healthy to get over your sickness. You see, the sane mind will not ask the insane question. But it's an insane mind that is asked to see that. Do you see?'

The sick mind is a burdened mind; the sick mind has become aware that it is burdened, and the sick mind says, 'What am I to do?' When the sick mind is aware that it is sick, it is already healthy. It is the mind that is unaware that it is sick that has the burden. But when the mind sees how very sick it is with all its burdens, and that sickness is an indication of the weight of the burden, then it is aware entirely of its sickness. Aware, which means there is no choice between sickness and health—it is sick. Then that awareness has its own activity which is completely different from the activity of sickness.

'But sir, there are many sick minds who realise that they are sick.'

That's it—part of them thinks they are healthy, another part thinks they are sick. It is not a total awareness of sickness. Total awareness is not an awareness of choice between health and sickness.

'Is it perhaps that we cling to the little piece that we have made as an island of sanity?'

That's right, exactly.

'And by separating that from the mass, which is the sick part, we perpetuate the illness.'

That is the whole issue. That is perfectly right.

18

WE TAKE A WRONG TURN
AND GET LOST

What goes wrong with people? They start, when they are very young, with such great hopes, with great enthusiasm and great interest, and as they grow older they seem to peter out; their ambitions become small, so obviously silly, making a name for themselves in the world, one way or another. Physically they go to seed and mentally they become duller and duller. What goes wrong?

He was rather short and there was a peculiar quality of trying to please. He knew several languages, had read a great deal and had been quite well off at one time. Now in his late 50s, he had put on considerable weight, was rather round-shouldered and full of years. Whenever you met him he would try to stand very straight, but it was an effort and in a few minutes he would go back to his usual posture.

From his rooms he had a rather nice view overlooking a large garden with an avenue of trees and the sparkling river beyond. It was a tropical river and it was lined with palm trees. From this height he overlooked the swaying palms, the waters, and a curving road that went past the noisy town, a temple and a school with shouting children.

When you first saw him in the old days he was very interested in religion, being very clever and bright. His religious outlook was not orthodox but somewhat revolutionary. He deeply wanted to find out. You would have said that he would devote his whole life to it, for he had given up many things that another would hold dear.

He had given up a good career too, for this, a career which

would have brought him quite a bit of money. He was married but somehow it didn't seem to play much part in his life. He had seven children but they were something he had produced in a dream. You felt that he was dissociated from them; though he took interest, it was rather an intellectual affair, not something that he felt profoundly.

And now those children had their own careers, their own lives, their own children. Probably he now saw them very rarely. It was like a man stretching out a hand to pat them on their shoulder, a kind of affectionate, distant recognition that they were his product, of a dim, past incident.

As he grew older, his religious fervour seemed to fade. The world was catching him. You could see that it was creeping into him. He was rather unaware of it. He wanted to be somebody in the religious world, whatever that may mean. Probably he would like to have been an archbishop, a representative of God or of some mystery; but that had slipped through his hands and faded. It had flattered him, as in a dream, what he could have been in a spiritual world which he had considered was worthwhile at one time. But now that was behind those high hills, rather barren and almost forgotten.

He wrote elaborate books exposing this or that in very complicated language, quoting in Sanskrit and discovering some new nuances of meaning in things forgotten. Those books sold fairly well but they didn't give him a name. He was hungering after the riches of renown, and again it didn't quite come off. You saw him between the intervals of the religious life and the literary life, and then he took to some mysterious paintings, full of colour, with deep significance. For him the mountain with the brilliant light of the evening sun was not just a mountain but was what lay behind it—the mystery, the symbol and the glory that was hidden. A tree wasn't a simple tree with its lovely branches and leaves—they were the product of 'Mother Earth, with heavy belly and bosom'. And a woman was the mother of all mothers, draped in fantastic robes of extravagant colours; a picture which nobody understood but the selected few. And so it went on. He said that people didn't appreciate the beauty of his paintings. He would like to have sold them; he said, 'I'll give you any number of them, if you will sell them.'

You saw him again several years later. He had put on more weight, had become more mysterious in himself, and now had cornered a certain aspect, a certain mystery, which he had discovered in the sacred Sanskrit literature. He was writing books about it but the hunger was still there. His friends were those who accepted all this. And now it was becoming a tragedy. Even if the house were burning, he was ready for whoever wanted to know the interpretation of some ancient riddle lost in obscure texts. The house was burning and he would talk about all this. But the hungry look, frustrated sorrow and the pain of fading life was in his eyes, of which probably he was not even aware. Or if he was aware, he was caught in the world that had given him nothing.

So what goes wrong with us? We start out with such great promise and we take a wrong turn and get lost in things that really don't matter at all. What went wrong with this man? Perhaps the word *wrong* isn't correct. What had clouded him? What had shut his eyes so that he no longer could see anything except the fulfilment of his own importance? What sorrow had bitten into his heart that he saw the light in his own shadow? He wouldn't want to talk to you, expose himself.

Was it the pride in his race, which he had never been able to put aside and now had caught up with him? Was it the empty well of his house, from which he was trying to drink? Or was it some fantastic ideal? He had dabbled with communism; he played with social utopia. Or was it that he had not loved anyone? That is it; that is the thing that destroys. Without that, you drink at a fountain whose waters never quench your thirst. He depended on the mystery of the word and his clever interpretation of it, and now he was emptyhanded, full of age, and looking down from the height of his room at life that has never touched his heart. That is it; that's what makes things go so colossally wrong, become so terrifyingly destructive. Cleverness, technology and the enthusiasm of social reform become the maturity of infants, without that one thing. That one thing you cannot find in books, through any painting or through the mystery of a symbol. And if you haven't that one thing, everything goes wrong. Then do what you will, nothing will come right.

19

THE INTELLECT IS VERY LIMITED

He was a Victorian, educated at one of the top universities. He was a heavily built man with sharp eyes which though they had a pleasant look had a certain kind of cruelty in them. He had been a priest in the distant past and now he was in the tropical climate, far from his parish, from the things that he had thought were important. He had come to India with a definite purpose. He liked the Indians but kept them at a distance. A few of them he tolerated in his room. Whenever he met them outside he was very polite, courteous, saluting them in their manner, but there was a sense of aloofness. You would find it hard to say that he was a cruel man but there was a streak of that in him. He was very reverential, a royalist and an authoritarian.

His reverence was increased or decreased in his hierarchical outlook. He had great respect for the kings and the queens of the world but was kindly tolerant to the servants, to the ordinary people he met on the road. If you were in his presence you were rather watchful not to say anything that might be wrong, that might not be just the right thing. You were cautious and he liked that. He would work all day long at the table, writing, dictating, and he had meetings, saw people, but there was always a distance between him and others, a distance that could probably never be bridged. Psychologically you would say he was completely ignorant. That ignorance gave a certain charm. He was heavily conditioned and one often wondered what his inner life was, if he had any, though he talked a great deal about it.

Inner life is an odd thing. It is not in proportion to the

outer life, though the outer and the inner meet. You may have wandered very far outwardly, throwing yourself into experience, gathering sensation, being well informed, but the inner life is not in proportion to that. Though the outer and the inner are one movement, the outward pilgrimage doesn't cover or penetrate into the deep inward life. However much you may acquire knowledge about the many things of the earth and of man, and correlate them all and have the capacity to narrate them in a book or on a platform or in your daily conversation, one wonders if this vast experience and knowledge will ever open the door to something that is not in the books and in the calculations of the mind.

The intellect is very limited for it is only a fragment of the whole expansive field of life. The cruelty and the decision of the intellect is not the inner life. He had meticulously worked out the inner life he talked about, even in diagrams. All that one had to do was just follow them and the doors of heaven would open.

There were many like him. There was that man who spoke a great deal on the radio about science; he guaranteed that if you did certain things you would find God within twelve years. Do this and do that and, voila, the magic. It was all so cut and dried, but done with great reverence. And if there was any conflict you just suppressed it, in the name of the highest. You just put away everything that wasn't right, locked it up with the key of decision and it would never appear again. Will, decision and the cutting out of all desire was the way to the beauty of life.

But somehow you liked him, and all that he said didn't mean very much. Probably he saw this too and presently he would drop you. When he met you he would show respect, but the wall of decision that separated you could never be climbed; you were on this side and he was on that side. And as he grew older all the old things returned, the church, the

Victorianism, the ritualism. The war only made it worse. He hated the enemy with real hatred and yet he talked about not hating. You wouldn't call it hypocrisy: if you hated the scorpion or poisonous snake you just killed it, and in the very killing of it you said, 'It poisons therefore it must be destroyed.' It was all in the pattern of decision. He was a good man, in the accepted sense of that word, but it was not a goodness that flowered.

He had a very clear mind, capable, efficient like a good machine, but there was something missing, the one thing that would have made all the difference in the world. What was it? He was well educated, had travelled a great deal, knew the world from a distance, lived an ascetic life satisfied with very little, frugal and refined, clean and abstemious, not crude. But yet there was something missing. It must have been missing from early in his life, like that man who was a scientist and had now become religious and guaranteed the beauty of God if you did certain things within a certain period of time. In all these human beings, when you looked at them and talked with them and walked with them, what was it that wasn't there, what perfume?

Was it the desire for power that destroyed them and distorted life? Was it this respect for the superior? Was it the obedience to a dedicated principle, concept or formula? Was it the deep-rooted egotism covered over by the glossy words of nobility? Was it 'the better' in the progress of becoming, the self-improvement, the time-binding quality of achievement? Was it the dedication to an ideal, personified or not? Was it the very desire to forget oneself that strengthened the self? Or was it the psychological evolution of one's own thought and the shoddiness of one's own being supposedly evolving into something marvellous; the pride of progress?

You saw the beauty of the earth and the light on the river and a fisherman going by, naked except for his loincloth. You looked out of the window but you never walked with the fisherman. You can identify yourself with the good and put away the evil, but this division and the wall of decision spoils your entire life.

20

THE POSITIVE APPROACH IS DESTRUCTIVE

She was married to a very rich man and was staying at the Ritz. She was what you might call a sophisticated person, educated, Catholic. She had done a lot of social work, had probably read a great many books, was quite intelligent, in the normal sense of that word, and quite serious. It is strange how such an intelligent mind with a clear-cut formula or a definite method could try to realise something that can never be approached through the intellectual or emotional way of life.

This phenomenon exists all over the world. They are very serious people who have worked hard, who have probably given up certain things for the good of society. They work tirelessly, carried on by their own interest and the realisation that something has to be done. They are absolutely convinced that you must have a method, as you have a method in business, in a political campaign, in a well-organised religious framework, or when you do something in the social world. All these have definite formulas laid down on well-known principles, clear, definite and purposive. In all these there is a direction, a positive assertion and clarification. They move always from the known to the known, feeling secure at each step, knowing where they are going, positive in their activity and in their goal. After all, education is the cultivation of the known into the known, moving from fact to fact, never deviating, never questioning fundamentally.

They are not materialistic, though they may be very rich. They have a suspicion of something more than physical wellbeing and are not entirely slaves to environment. They have worked hard, they have fought hard and their outlook is hard too. You meet such people all over the world, not only well-cultured individuals, but who are alive to the disasters that are going on, to the mess the politicians are making through their personal vanity or for the importance of their party. They are also aware of the great disturbance that is going on within the pattern of religious organisations and the general havoc that war and the narrow spirit breed. They are highly intellectual or devastatingly emotional but moving in the same direction: the reformation of the world and vague aspirations of a spiritual life.

It is the positive approach to life. It is a mind that must see everything very clearly as it goes along to the very end. The end must be as clear, definite and precise as the beginning. And in this positive clarity, discipline becomes a subtle form of conformity, which denies freedom. Yet they feel this very positive approach offers freedom. This approach is really materialistic—their gods, their utopias, social reform and activities are for good; goodness that must be known, virtue that must be practised. Evolution is the final movement of life; the everlasting becoming better and better and better.

This positive approach, which promises so much, is fundamentally the most destructive, for in it there is no freedom at all, neither at the beginning nor at the end. The total negation of all this is one of the most difficult things to comprehend. Denying all systems and methods that promise freedom, is freedom. The emptying the mind of the positive, which is the formula, the ideal, the pursuit of the utopia, is the most positive action, in which alone a fundamental revolution can take place. The beauty of this is not immediately perceptible. What is immediately perceptible for a positive mind are the rungs of the ladder, and when there is no ladder to climb it gets lost. The fear of losing a grip on the ladder sustains inventing new ladders. You hear this on every occasion, among the Hindus, the Catholics and the communists. They start from a central thesis or a belief and weave their cloth round it, and that very cloth blinds them.

There is really no division between the positive and the negative. It is not going from this to that but awareness of the implications of the positive that inevitably brings the other about; the total perception of the so-called positive, in which is included systems, methods, self-improvement, the gradual process of achievement, the movement from the known to the known. Total perception of the so-called positive is the total negation of all that, and this negation has its own radical movement.

21

LIFE CANNOT BE RULED BY IDEAS

You meet them all over the world, in the most unexpected places, and you are rather surprised when you do. They have more or less the same jargon, the same authority, the same verbal explanations, and a whole list of patients waiting for them. One met them in a remote corner of India, leading a group of people who seemed so excited about it. Under a tree on a lawn they come and sit with you and discuss analysis. They are astonishingly of more or less the same pattern, somewhat odd, and most of them are well-to-do.

They have their gurus, their doctors who have analysed a great many people, and themselves have gone through a period of analysis, generally very keenly. They have come to this out of their own confusion and one feels they are still confused though they have new formulas, and they want to help others with it. As you meet them you feel their assurance. They are certain. They are quick with words and explanations. They have an air of authority arrived at through a great deal of struggle, experience and investigation, and have somehow mastered themselves. It appears that they expect you to honour them; they expect your attentive acknowledgement of their superiority, your deference to their authority and maturity. It is like a beautiful building with very little light inside; a structure of words, explanations and successes. They all have success; their patients make them and without the patients they would be lost. The façade they present is not very stable; behind it you see their anxiety, their aggressiveness, their fears and the obstinacy of anger. They are like everybody else only they have a new instrument in their hands, and the instrument has become all-important.

Again, you meet them in all parts of the world, on the sunlit road leading to the river, dignified, alone, in a saffron robe, clean, having one meal a day, preaching here and there, or silently walking from one village to another. Or they hold classes on the Gita, and chant to large audiences. Or they have ashrams where they train their disciples to meditate, to work socially, to collect money, to print books. Or they live alone in a distant village among the mountains, not saying a word for fifteen years. In their solitude they are physically alone but are never alone in themselves. You meet them in monasteries, with dark robes and bright sashes, getting up very early in the morning and praying, cultivating the fields and the vineyards, strictly obeying the vows they have taken.

Or there are those who have left all this and abandoned the monastery, the religious orders, but remain conditioned as monks. And there is the priest who is doing good work in his parish, struggling with the poor, trying to make their life a little more happy. The missionary, the monk, the priest and the sannyasi are wedded to their formulas, conditioned by the culture around them, but inwardly they are like other human beings, incomplete, living with despair, loneliness. They are aggressive, immovable in their faith, driven by ideas.

You meet them everywhere, the intellectual trying to reshape the world according to a new political or religious theory. Often they are tall, thin, nervous, burning with the peculiar energy of a mind full of ideas. The corridor of ideas leads to darkness and the intellectuals realise it at one time or another. Then they join the church or take up some Eastern philosophy or belief, which is for them a form of suicide. There are others who actually end their lives.

You observe all this, the psychologist, the monk and the intellectual, and you see that idea and theory dominate. What should be is most important; the verbal structure and the immense importance given to the understanding of the word. They perceive the shallowness of knowledge when it is too late and then turn to faith as a way out of their verbal confusion. This is the strange part of it; harmony of life is not in the verbal assertion, in the endless theory of what should be, or in the ideal. They live in a different world, though they talk about this world. Somehow you feel that sorrow is with them. Their meditation, their analysis, their intellectual capacity does not dispel this thing. They paint, they write books, they love music, they know the artists and write beautiful poems, but the weight of sorrow is with them. They live in a world of ideas, formulas, theories.

Life is not that. Life cannot be ruled by ideas or shaped according to ideas. So sorrow continues. Wisdom is not in the world of formulas and theories but only in the ending of sorrow.

22

IS CREATION DIFFERENT
FROM EXPRESSION?

'I would like to ask a very simple question. I know many artists fairly well, not only painters and musicians but also writers and sculptors. They talk about expression, putting down things on paper, using their hands in the carving of marble or writing a poem. To them expression is part of creation. It is creation for them and without that expression they feel frustrated. They are not satisfied with what they painted yesterday and they want to create and express something new. This is my question: is expression creation, or does creation have nothing whatsoever to do with expression?'

Self-expression is the negation of creation. When the self demands expression, in whatever form, whether it is in the art world, in the business world or in the family world, it is not creation. It is a form of egotistic activity, self-interest, which may enlarge, glorify the 'me', and that is not creation.

Self-expression demands recognition by society, and society if you observe it very closely is the self-expression of millions. When an artist is concerned with self-expression he is really concerned with social acceptance of what he puts on the canvas or has made to fit into the pattern of a particular society. Self-expression is never in the field of freedom and an artist who is not free is no longer an artist.

'So what is the difference between self-expression and creation?'

Let us be concerned first with that word creation—*to create, to build, to give birth to. If that has any tinge or touch of the self, it is no longer a movement of creation, for the self is always limited, isolated. It divides. Where there is division between me and you, we and they, there is no building together. When there is movement in which there is no fragmentation as the 'me' and the 'you', as expression and not expression, or creation and not creation, that is creation. That is real creation.*

Perhaps we shouldn't use that word at all; it is something beyond all words and measure. But we will use it for the sake of convenience and verbal understanding. What has creation to do with an artist who is concerned with self-fulfilment, frustration, recognition, value, position, prestige, jealousy, fame? What has that to do with the other? How can the two come together? How can darkness come into light or light into darkness? It cannot. The artist who is using the instrument for his own glory, for his own fame or for the gathering of money needs self-expression, whether he is completely in isolation or in the limelight of the world. One wonders why there is this demand for expression at all. Living, in the sense we are talking about, is part of expression. You don't separate living from expression. When you are not living, in the total sense of movement in that word, then you cling to expression; then expression becomes extraordinarily important. But when there is this total movement of life and living and the sense of beauty, love and death, expression becomes a very insignificant part of it; you may express or not express. But when you emphasise expression then you are lost in the world of conflict.

Emphasis on expression is the denial of beauty. The word individual *means indivisible, whole, integral, but the emphasis on expression and the demand for expression is from one who is in himself broken up, fragmentary, divided. Division is not individuality. When there is no division, which is the true meaning of the individual, there is no sorrow and there is not this incessant demand for expression or self-expression. When there is the absence of the self, expression or non-expression becomes extraordinarily trivial.*

23

HOW WE WASTE OUR LIFE!

They were marching in a long procession, the generals with their decorations, bright uniforms, plumed hats, brass breastplates, swords and spurs; the lady in her carriage all dressed up, surrounded by soldiers, more uniforms coming on behind, top hats. People stood gaping at them. They would have liked to be in that procession. If you strip these people of their uniforms, their feathers and their grand-sounding names, they will be like the people standing by the roadside, gaping nobodies. It is the same everywhere: the name, the position, the prestige are what matter. The writer, the artist, the musician, the director, the head of a big company; strip them of their outward show and their small status then what is left? There are these two things, function and status. Function is exploited to achieve status. Confusion arises when we give status to function, and yet they are always overlapping. The cook is looked down upon and the man in uniform is respected. In this procession we are all caught, disrespect for the one and respect for the other.

One wonders if one stripped oneself of the status, the glamour of titles, the furniture, the dead memories, what actually would be left. If one has capacity, that cannot be minimised. However, if such capacity is used to achieve position, power, status, then the mischief begins. The capacity is exploited for money, position, status. If one has no capacity, one may even then have status through money, family, hereditary or social circumstances. All this is vulgarity. We are part of it. What makes us so vulgar, so common and cheap? This ugliness is directly proportionate to the amount of status. Everyone gaping at this endless procession is us. The onlooker who gapes creates the status which he admires, so does the queen in the golden carriage. Both are equally vulgar.

Why are we caught in this stream? Why do we take part in this? The audience is as much responsible for the spectacle as the people strutting on the stage. We are the actors and the audience. When we object to the show of status, it is not that we repudiate status but rather that we attach importance to it; we would like to be there on the stage ourselves—'or at least my son...' We read all this and perhaps smile ironically or bitterly, reflecting on the vanity of the spectacle, but we watch the procession. Why can't we, when we look at it, really laugh and throw it all aside? To throw it all aside we must throw it all aside within ourselves, not only outside.

That is why one leaves the world and becomes a monk or sannyasi. But there too there is peculiar status, position and illusion. The society makes the sannyasi and the sannyasi is the reaction to society. There too is the vulgarity and the parade. Would there be a monk if there were no recognition of the monk? Is this accolade of recognition any different from the recognition of the generals? We are all in this game and why are we playing it? Is it the utter inward poverty, the total insufficiency in ourselves, which neither book nor priests nor gods nor any audience can ever fill? Neither your friend nor your wife can fill it. Is it that we are afraid of living with the past, with death?

How we waste our life! In the procession or out of the procession we are always of it, as long as this aching void remains. This is what makes us vulgar, frightened, and so we become attached and depend. And the whole strife of the procession goes on whether you are in it or admiring from the grandstand. To leave it all is to be free of this emptiness. If you try to leave it or determine to leave it you cannot, for it is yourself. You are of it, so you cannot do anything about it.

The negation of this vulgarity which is yourself is freedom from this emptiness. This negation is the act of complete inaction with regard to emptiness.

24

ALL SEEKING IS FROM EMPTINESS AND FEAR

You will find him on the banks of the Ganges, dirty, naked, emaciated, fierce, plastered with mud and covered with beads. He has taken a vow never to wash, never to talk, never to comb his long matted hair. He has become little more than an animal, angry and sly.

You will find him higher up the river, clean, elegantly garbed in silk, serious, somewhat sophisticated and scholarly, discoursing to an ecstatic group of disciples. You will find him alone, very clean, wearing a robe of saffron with a staff in his hand, keeping aloof, dignified, slender, glowingly healthy. He will hardly talk to you and when he does there is a ring in his voice. His eyes are clear and have a quality of distinction. There is austerity, chastity and beauty.

You will find him in that big house with hundreds of disciples of every kind—lawyers, retired judges, famous film stars from the East and West. He knows Sanskrit and can quote the ancient Vedas, explaining what truth is and how to meditate. Without exactly saying so, he makes it quite clear that he is in daily communication with God. He can put in a good word for you. There is also an unwritten contract that if you do certain things according to his prescriptions he may take you to God after a great many years.

You will find her in another big house with thousands of disciples from all over the world. She is garlanded by her disciples who also bathe and feed her, putting the food into her mouth for she is too unworldly to eat herself and lives on another plane of consciousness. Or so they say. Is it ecstasy, is it hysteria, is it hallucination? The disciples are all in a dither, carrying on around her with fruit, flowers, incense, cymbals and drums. For hours on end they hypnotically chant her name, clapping their hands.

You will find him in a dirty little room with rats and mice playing under the bed upon which he sits, a bloated figure, unshaven, dirty. There is an unhealthy faraway expression on his face. He is a great scholar. Brahmins come from all over to sit at his holy feet. He knows the scriptures intimately and can quote them for hours. Chocolate wrappers lie among the books on the floor and mice eat the crumbs.

You will find him sitting in a cave. There is a beautiful look on his face. He is witty but seems to have little to say. Disciples sit around him in silence and that very silence seems to solve all their problems. Of course there is always the battle for position and power next to the great man.

You will find her running a very efficient, quite prosperous colony of disciples. People come from far to see the school, the waterworks and the printing press. She seems so frail but everybody fears and obeys. She rules their most intimate lives with a rod of iron.

You will find him clad in black or resplendent in scarlet in Rome, slowly dying in his belief, his practices, his rituals and dogmas. He is about God's business. God will not be unappreciative; one day he might make him a bishop or a pope. All the gorgeous rituals, jewels, austerities, and the quiet security of having found the only right way in this well-established tradition are his. There is wealth, power, knowledge, the sanctity of time. He is in the cathedrals, in the local parish church, in the protestant pulpit, in the big house on Park Avenue. He is scattered all over the world converting, correcting, persuading. He has persuaded more or less forcefully according to the political opportunities of the time and place. He starts schools, hospitals and various other good works.

He is of every shade and colour in all parts of the world, trying every conceivable trick to capture God. He becomes a Hindu or a Catholic or a Buddhist, or goes into a monastery to meditate on words. Or he wonders endlessly how some duck got into some bottle. He is always seeking God, truth, a promised heaven, a beauty not of the earth, an ecstasy which does not fade, an experience which is transcendental, a peace which passes all understanding, a love which encompasses all.

And life goes by.

Strangely all these people seem to be more or less the same person but in different garbs, with different phrases on their lips, playing different tricks, having different formulas or beliefs.

And life goes by.

What is it they all want? They want to realise something which is not of this world. For this world has made them lonely, empty, unhappy, mediocre. Some think they have achieved, realised, experienced; and they are willing to teach you for a price, pecuniary or psychological. They know and you don't know. Their knowing is their decay. Those who say they know, whether in Rome, Benares, Mecca, Tokyo, New York or Moscow, are all the product of environment, and what they know is what their ignorance longed to know. Therefore what they know is their ignorance. The realisation of their Atman is already the known. The word of Christ is valid to them only because they have been conditioned to believe it is. The Muslim with his obstinate dogmatism is impenetrable, and the Hindu and the Buddhist and the Christian are the same.

Is this the way we find truth? Is this the way to the supreme? Why is it that they are all so clever and highly intellectual, with extraordinary cunning traditional arguments? Why is it that they have not questioned all this? Why is it that they accept authority at all? To tread the path of another is to walk in their shadow. In the shadow or in the symbol you can never find light. They will argue with you but they will never let go of their anchorage, for if they do, all the structure holding them together will collapse. They are frightened. It is this fear that makes them believe, search, practise, meditate, that makes them concerned about love and finding God. So this fear is everywhere.

Fear is this emptiness which is in each one of us and we try to fill it with innumerable recipes for God, good works, divine knowledge, worldly knowledge, amusement and entertainment, religious or otherwise. But it is always there, this emptiness and fear.

So in their emptiness they practise for something which their fear has conceived to be great and they remain in emptiness. Strip them of all their jargon, robes, formulas and holy certainties and what remains? Dull, aching emptiness and the fear of being nothing. The beauty of life goes by. Can you and I go beyond this seeking, these tortures, these actions of emptiness and fear? If not we are bound to walk in darkness. In darkness there is no light of understanding. Light is not at the end of fear and darkness; it is here when you know how to look. To see is the greatest thing.

The activity of all seeking is from emptiness and fear. Seeing this is to put it all aside. The hope of finding is less important than the reason why we seek. When we see that this seeking is out of emptiness and fear it has no more meaning, but will that emptiness and fear now express itself in some other way? If so you are back on the banks of the Ganges, though it may be a nightclub this time. If the emptiness and fear no longer express in any way at all, is there any emptiness and fear left? It is the running away and the covering up that perpetuates it.

Is there another activity which is not of emptiness and fear? Is there a way of life which itself is sacred? If it is to be found, it is *here* in the actions of relationship that is all our living, and not over there. Love is here not there. And the beauty of the leaf is this love.

25

CAN I STOP DECLINE IN MYSELF?

There he was, the grey man. He was grey all over. In his walk, in the posture of his body, in the droop of his head, there was something very wrong. You saw strain, anger, arrogance, cunning. Psychologically he was like an animal at bay, crouching, ready to spring. There was fear, fatigue and anger. He came from some ancient caste of India and was very proud of it. He somehow managed to carry over the particular arrogance of this background into Western surroundings and clothes. His trousers were rolled up and he shuffled in his carpet slippers. The eye was hard and the voice was inclined to whine. It conveyed the subtlest inflections of flattery or threat according to who you were or what he wanted of you at the time. He treated you to a repertoire of fixed attitudes of mind and body and you knew you were expected to respond in a certain way. His whole being was hardened and brittle.

You could not talk to him about anything without his getting angry. He was a most frustrated man. On occasion, perhaps when he had had a couple of drinks, his attitude would become confidential and sentimental. He must have been quite nice when he was young. People said he played jokes but even those were a bit strange. There was in them something cruel, nagging and bullying. This picture of a man was hardness, coldness, calculation, cruelty and bitterness. One also saw that he had suffered much himself; it was as if he now bore the marks of all his own aggressions. The eyes that once flashed black were now grey and lifeless. He was a broken man and managed to convey quite clearly that it was your fault.

How has all this happened? Was it his fault or yours?

Was it the environment or was the seed of corruption already there? What went wrong? Was it his high hopes that could not be realised? Very few people ever had so much opportunity, encouragement, education and freedom. He had not wanted to be second to anybody. Now he was behind everybody. What had happened? How we waste our life! We do make mistakes, tell lies, get angry, run after women, but this doesn't destroy us. We can change these things and we should and we do. But this man was irredeemable. What had gone wrong?

We destroy ourselves by our moods, our elation, our deep depression. We are too proud to examine ourselves or to let others examine us. We resist criticism. We cut ourselves off from any relationship that might open the door to our own mind and heart. We become so cunning in our resistance that it gets better with age. We manage to make everything someone else's fault. We pick on someone else's faults to mask our own. We become deeply suspicious, and every remark, every action, has a double meaning. One grows more and more secretive, lonely, isolated. Could all this have been prevented? Who is to prevent it, the world, or me, or you?

Can I prevent my own destruction? Can I not destroy myself? When I don't destroy myself, I don't destroy another. How can I stop decline in myself? This wave of degeneration is always upon me; there isn't a moment's respite. How is this to be stopped? Does one ever ask this question, or does one only ask it when the bell has already tolled? Then of course it is too late. When is the moment to ask this question? The irredeemable cannot ask this question. He can confess, propitiate all the gods imaginable, make amends, be deeply contrite, but all this is the action of a man who is already dead. It is too late. So one asks oneself when is the moment to stay the corruption? Is it in youth? When is it too late?

It has nothing to do with age, time or circumstances. It is

Can I stop decline in myself?

because we rely on age, time, circumstances and opportunity that we are destroyed. This dependence is the seed of destruction.

We rely on things outside for fulfilment. This fulfilment never comes. This grey man comes instead. We blame the world for this greyness because the world is grey. But it is grey because we, you and I and everybody, have made it so. We are blaming ourselves; I am blaming myself outside for what I am inside. There is only one entity not two. I am blaming myself but I don't know it. I am responsible for my own ruin. So I am cursing myself, and rightly so, but I don't know it is myself! So what am I to do?

The ruin is there screaming at me. It seems to have come from outside, but the outside is made by the inside and is the same. I am the generator of it all. What can I do? What can you do? Can you ask this question of yourself and really mean it? When you ask this question you have the energy and the earnestness. In asking this question you put all the other circumstances aside—time, age, the world. In this there is no morbidity, depression or hope. You are faced with something enormous. When you are challenged by something so enormous you have the energy to respond. Because you are absolutely sure that you are responsible for everything yourself, you stop decaying.

You have blamed the world and others. This has taken great energy and ruined you. You stop blaming others. This energy is there now. This concentration of energy is the beginning of the end of decline. This energy is not mine or the world's. It is intelligence.

26

AT WHAT DEPTH
DO YOU WANT ORDER?

It was a morning full of enchantment. The sky was intensely blue after heavy rains. The river was flowing with a great deal of noise which filled the valley. The snow-capped mountains stood extraordinarily clearly against the blue sky. There was incredible freshness, as though the earth was just born, and you were looking with eyes that had never seen those mountains before. The meadows, the hills and the mountains seemed to fill the whole sky and the earth, expanding endlessly. The sun was just touching the peaks of the mountains and the snow up there was turning pink.

The valley lay in shadow, remembering the light of yesterday. Soon the sun would fill it and the noise of the day would begin. But as you watched the sun on those peaks, so light and delicate, you became as light and delicate, and the beauty of it filled you. You were part of everything and you were not separate from that light on those peaks and the noise of the river. It was really an extraordinarily beautiful morning, full of promise.

A magpie flew off the pine and joined its mate in the field just below you. They were very shy but were talkative amongst themselves. If you came near they either flew away or became quite still. They were rather vicious birds, killing the little mice and birds.

He was a youngish man, well dressed, sparing in his gestures. He had a pleasant voice and a good turn of phrase that pleased him probably more than a good meal. 'I don't think I understand,' he said. 'You use words that have special meaning and may have no meaning to me at all. You seem to give a particular nuance or emphasis to words, which I miss. Whilst I try to understand what you are saying you are already off with other set of words and ideas. Perhaps it would be helpful if you could stick to one or two ideas or issues and go into them pretty thoroughly.

'I am a very disturbed man, perhaps a little more than others, but I have not been to an analyst. I am disturbed about my family, my relationship with my wife, with my job, and I'm generally discontent with things as they are. How am I to bring order in my life and in myself, given this mounting discontent and the unhappiness it is bringing about? I want to live, if it is possible in this mad world, a sane and orderly life.'

At what depth do you want order? Do you want it at a superficial level or at the very roots of your being? Do you want order at work separate from the family, which again is different from the order within yourself? Do you want fragmentary order or a total order? Fragmentary order, order broken-up, is followed by disorder.

What does the word order *mean? There is order that gives one satisfaction, comfort and a sense of security. There is the order of resistance, behind which there might be disorder. There is order in the environment, over there, and order here in yourself. Established order becomes a habit and so one lives mechanically.*

'For me, order is a state of mind which is not easily disturbed; living a regular, orderly, well-balanced life. Order is not a following of a pattern day after day but it is active, driving and overcomes difficulties, emotional or otherwise. I want order outwardly and also I would like to have a fairly good semblance of order inwardly. I use the word *semblance* because I really don't know what it means to live a truly orderly life without it becoming monotonous, stupid and worthless. An orderly life according to a blueprint is obviously a stupid way of life. I have known disorder, contradiction and the meanness of life.'

The more a life is disorderly, contradictory, confusing, the greater the neurotic state of the brain. The brain needs order but not the order of conformity. It is only when it is functioning freely without any disturbance, without contradiction, that the brain establishes its own order. Such a brain is healthy, objective, non-emotional, living with facts and not with opinions or with the dead memories of yesterday. Such a brain brings about in its relationships a quality of order that does not breed confusion, disorder and misery.

Can there be social order without having order within oneself? The social disorder with its injustice is the product of our own disorder, of our own inward confusion. Emphasising social order will not put an end to inward disorder. Surely the two must go together, not as separate movements. Sir, as we asked, at what level of one's being does one want order?

That word is rather ugly, militaristic and tyrannical.

The dictators want order and so does the military—precise, regular, respectable and conforming. Anything that does not come into this design is considered disorderly. The tyrant, the dictator would destroy those who brought about disorder in what he considers to be orderly, what he considers to be social good, suppressing any form of freedom which might bring disorder.

Seeing all this, the various demands and expressions of order, the extraordinary order of the universe and the great disorder of human beings, can the brain evolved in confusion and conditioned to accept the chaos and misery, free itself and in the very freeing itself from disorder bring about its own order?

Disorder can never give space in which goodness can flower. The very essence or root of disorder is self-centred movement or activity—the 'me' that is constantly isolating itself, building a wall of resistance around itself of conformity, acceptance and denial. This yielding 'me' with its ambitions, comparisons, aspirations, aggression and competitiveness brings about disorder with its self-centred activity. This is what is happening outwardly in society *and also inwardly within the structure of one's own thought, memories and intentions. Where there is this activity there is no space for the birth of a new thing. Freedom and space become an idea, something to be achieved or striven after by the 'me'. This destroys that freedom in which alone order can be.*

The brain needs order so that it can function without any distortion, without any resistance, freely and fully. To function it must have space and this space is denied when the self operates.

'I came here to have some kind of order and you are offering me something which is so destructive of my daily life that I am frightened of it and I am not at all sure that I want it. What I really want is some comfort in life, to deceive myself with an ordinary image of myself. But you remove all images, pointing out that any image is the product of thought. Probably I will continue in my disorder with my discontent, hoping that the seed you have shown me flowers without my knowing it. When that happens I know I shall have to face it.'

You are trying to postpone to a future date what can and must be faced now. In the now *there is no future. It is there for you to look. Don't invent the future but rather be honest and say, 'I do not want to look.' That is much more sane and rational than saying to yourself, 'I hope to have the courage in the future to look at the fact,' which only leads to a great deal of deception and hypocrisy.*

27

WISDOM DOES NOT COME THROUGH PRACTICE

He had that strange pride of having achieved what he set out for. Added to that was pride in leading a respectable, righteous life. He said he had been a vegetarian all his life, never drank or smoked, and his sexual life was limited to his wife. He was fairly well dressed and seemed prosperous. When he sat down he assumed a pose which was quite natural to him. He was somewhat respectful but with a far-off feeling of condescension. He was full of words and gestures with the strange sense of arrogance that comes with a great deal of knowledge and achievement. He said he had written books and was surprised that we had not read them. He took it for granted that he was well known.

'I am a Buddhist. I practise the teachings; I have been to several monasteries and practise meditation and awareness. I see that you talk a great deal about awareness and attention. I suppose you practise it too and I would like to ask where you learned it or from what book you have gathered all that you talk about. I have attended one of your talks and that interested me quite a bit. What does awareness mean to you?'

Before we go into that, isn't it strange that we never ask why we call ourselves Buddhists, Sufis or Christians? Why do we belong to anything at all, to any group, to any nationality or sect? We are human beings with all our troubles and miseries. There is pride in the assertion of belonging to something secretly or openly, setting us apart, dividing us. It is like a man who says he is a communist, as though that were the ultimate achievement. It gives a certain distinction. So the label becomes far more important than the human being. This is very destructive of all human relationships since it denies love.

The awareness of which you speak I have not read or practised or learned from another. This is said with no pride but merely as a fact. Perhaps you will be good enough to explain what you mean by awareness, what you have learned from your books and practices. Then perhaps together we can see the truth or falseness of what it is to be aware.

'What I have learned from practice and reading is to be attentive to the bodily activity, from watching the movement of the toe to the movement of the eye and thought; watching as I take a step, how I sit and how I eat; watching the manner of my speech and so on. You practise this for several hours a day and may fall asleep but you are rudely awakened. Gradually after several weeks or even months you begin to be aware of the organism and the entity that controls the organism, the overall entity that is the watcher of the watched. It gives you a tremendous sense of accuracy, control and the joy of being highly disciplined.

As you penetrate deeper you have that strange awareness of utter silence, which personally I have not been able to capture yet. This is only part of awareness which I have practised but of course there are wider and deeper aspects which exist in Zen and other forms of meditation. All this may convey verbally very little but I am quite sure you will agree with most of this.'

Agreement and opinion are one thing but the actual is another. The one leads to bondage and confusion and the other to the flowering of goodness. We must deal with facts, not with what somebody has said, no matter who it is. What is important is to see for ourselves, not to follow the footsteps of another hoping it will lead to the highest. Following another, however great, is the ending of awareness and of the beauty of love. Could we this morning at least, put aside the authority of another and find out for ourselves non-verbally—though we must use words to communicate—what it means to be aware, and see where it leads? There must be freedom to perceive, and not the image of perception.

'Are you asking me to put aside all my knowledge, my book-reading, the authorities I have worshipped, including the sacred ones?'

Of course, sir. Otherwise, if we may point out, you are only repeating what someone else has said. Awareness is part of the rejection of authority, however promising and satisfying it may seem.

'Isn't this rather sacrilegious? And supposing I am capable of doing this, wouldn't all the knowledge which I have acquired interfere constantly with perception of the actual?'

Of course it would, and therefore what is important is to be aware of this knowledge which is interfering.

'How can I be aware of it and at the same time separate myself from it?'

It depends on how you are aware of it. Either you are aware of it as an observer and the knowledge is the thing observed, in which there is division, or there is awareness without the division of the observer and observed. It is this awareness we are talking about, not the awareness of an observer who says, 'This knowledge interferes with observing and therefore what am I to do with it? How can I suppress it, resist it or live with it?' That maintains the division. One has to begin to be aware of this division and see the full significance of it. The very seeing it is the end of this division. As long as the observer is separate, awareness is broken up as the observer who examines and the thing observed, struggling with it, suppressing it or overcoming it, and so always sustaining division with its conflicts. Most of us remain at that level. This is said with no derogatory feeling.

'Are you then saying it is the division that is the root of the trouble?'

That is only part, and a fairly obvious part, of what it is to be aware. The existence of this division, becoming aware of it and the ending of it, are part of awareness. When this happens it is not as an idea that it should happen in order to achieve greater awareness—for awareness is not progressive; it is not first this and then that. When there is awareness of this division and what is implied in the division—the conflict, the choice, the confusion and so on—then there is the perception that the observer is the observed. In this perception there is a complete revolution in awareness. Then there is a vast sea of awareness, not as yours or mine but an awareness in which there is the total absence of the 'me' and the thought of 'me' and the thought which has projected the 'me'—there is no shore from which the observer can watch the sea.

'But this is impossible for me to achieve because I am not even aware of the first division.'

Yet you have for many years been practising awareness. One should have thought the first question would have been: who is aware and what is it he is aware of? Doesn't this show the absurdity of systems, methods and practices? Intelligence is much more important than the method. The most unintelligent can practise a method and remain foolish. Wisdom does not come through practice. Intelligence is not sharpened in the routine of daily practice. Seeing what practice and method imply is the beginning of intelligence which is understanding.

So one strips oneself of all the labels of Buddhist, Christian, Hindu, and faces the reality of the human being—the sorrow, the passing pleasures, the anxiety, fear and so on—that come to an end in the light of awareness. Until this is done in the forward movement of the energy that takes different forms of destructive, assertive, self-centred activity, then awareness is merely a plaything for those who want to be entertained religiously or philosophically.

'You know, sir, my studies have made me very serious. I would be considered a serious man. But after what I have heard I find myself at a loss. I find I have nothing. I thought I had achieved a great deal after these years of struggle but now I find I am where I started, ignorant of myself and of my arrogance and the darkness of my mind in which there is no love. From now on I will not call myself anything and will begin without ever seeking an ending.'

28

THE BRAIN NEEDS
COMPLETE SECURITY

You went across the rickety bridge and took a path that goes by the ancient well. That well is supposed to be many thousands of years old. A few women were drawing water from it, talking endlessly. You passed by the well and went along under the tamarind trees, taking a meandering, well-trodden path among the fields, passing mango groves, ruined temples and a monk who lives nearby a well-looked-after temple. A little further along there is an ancient village. They say it existed before the Buddha, over three thousand years old. Now it is neglected, dirty, squalid. Children play in the dusty streets and open sewers run by. There were cells where pilgrims could stay during the night if they wished. This village, by its very old age, is respected as something very holy; it is on the road of pilgrimage.

You left all that behind and took another path past some more ancient temples in ruins, mango groves, tamarind and green fields. There was poverty everywhere—the degradation of it; the utter callousness of people to their environment, to the beauty of the land and the extraordinary open sky. Just beyond was the river. One hesitates to call it a river—rivers are so common, there are so many of them all over the world, passing through towns, polluted; and every river has a name. This one is somehow the mother of all rivers. It should not have a name. It comes from the Himalayas, down through valleys, past towns and villages and open spaces. Here, as you watched it, as you saw the current go by, it had become completely anonymous. It is just water with a great depth, going by, flowing by. Watching it that evening you felt you were going with it far away; and the heavens and earth were part of the river. The beauty of it made you completely silent.

'I have been a socialist for many years. I work for it. It is very important that the world should become socialistically minded. I am not of the extreme left; I'm not a communist though I have read Marx. There are many things which are true in what he says. I remain a confirmed socialist: my father was socialist, my friends are, the group around me are.

'I heard you saying in your talk that systems, including mine, only divide people into organised groups, quarrelling with each other, wasting their energies arguing which theory or system is the best. You also said that the system and the concern over the system is not going to feed the people, is not going to make the villager happy, give him food, educate him. I think you are wrong. We need systems. We have to have some kind of pattern in action, a guideline, an ideal around which most of us can gather and devote ourselves to. Apparently you are against all systems.'

Systems divide people; you have your system, another his system. One is a communist, another a socialist or a capitalist, and each group is convinced that his own particular pattern or formula is more important than the other. In this battle, in this division, the main purpose is not only forgotten but entirely neglected. The system becomes far more important than the people. Here in this land with vast population, ignorance, disease and despairing poverty, why can't all of you, belonging to various groups, drop your systems, your particular ideologies, your conceits and ambitions—the desire for power, prestige and all the rest of it—and all get together to see that the people have food, clothes and proper shelter? This can be done if all of us forget our ambitious, personal identification with a system and put all that aside. Why can't we, every one of us, work to bring about a happy people on this lovely earth, so that we can live at peace with beauty and love?

'That is exactly what we want to do. We also want what you say we must have; and our system is the best. Communism with its tyranny and bureaucracy destroys people; there is no freedom. And the extreme right becomes fascist, inevitably. So we feel that we are more capable of giving an opportunity to the people to work, to live, to abide in peace.'

That's just it, sir. You have your method and you cling to that method, to that ideal, and the communist does exactly the same. He has it all well thought out; he offers his method, and so there you are. To you, the method, the system is far more important, far more significant than forgetting your socialism, communism or capitalism and getting together to stop wars, to feed the people, to see that people are happy, well educated. That is not your concern. Your concern is over the system and so you must everlastingly divide, bring about conflict and misery and confusion. This is so simple and obvious but I know that you will carry on with your socialism because each one identifies himself with a system, with a method, with the ideal. It offers him an opportunity for his vanity, for his ambition, for his energy. He would rather sacrifice the greater for the lesser. He is not concerned with the whole of man.

This problem of poverty, war and division of nationalities, division of religions, division of political and economic groups, is going to destroy the world. When one realises this, actually sees it with one's eyes and hears it with one's heart, then systems of any kind are irrelevant, have no meaning. What is relevant, what is material, what is significant is that we all, every human being, get together and see, not in some distant future as an ideal, but actually see that this thing is done, and to see that one has the energy, the drive, the urgency. One must forget or set aside all systems, all methods, all divisions as communist, socialist, capitalist, the Asian or the Westerner. All that must be set aside, for systems do not cleanse the mind or empty the heart of the things of the mind.

'I understand what you are saying about systems and the divisions they make in the world. I will have to feel my way into it and perhaps one of these days give it up. But that means I have not only to fight with my friends but also to separate myself from all the work that I have done. I will have to go into that and see what can be done.

'I want to ask another question. You said yesterday morning that human beings are conditioned not only by the religious, political and economic conditionings, but by the conditioning of the culture, the society in which we live and have lived for thirty million years. You pointed out that this is not only at the periphery but deep down; the whole consciousness and the brain cells themselves are heavily conditioned. You said that there will be no peace in the world unless this conditioning is understood and we break through the heavy walls of tradition. You explained very carefully that this conditioning is the result not only of time but of the race, of the family, of the environment in which the particular mind of the human has lived.

'It is difficult for me to understand how a mind which is so heavily and terribly conditioned can free itself from the past so entirely that the very brain cells themselves become new. Of course, you are not saying this as a theory or speculative ideal. From what you said it is very clear that this can be done and it should be done. So I would like to go into it rather deeply. First, the possibility of such a thing seems incredibly difficult.'

If I may interrupt you, possibility *is rather an odd word. What is possible can be done or has already been done. That is fairly simple. If a man has climbed a mountain, another can climb it. It is possible. The possible has already been accomplished, done. If you are thinking in terms of possibility, the possibility becomes very small, very limited. We surround ourselves with what is possible and so we remain with easy achievement, success, gain and so on. What is of far greater importance is to see what is* impossible; *then in relation to that impossibility the possible becomes far greater and therefore far more demanding, far more urgent. The impossible is possible, but the possibility becomes a thing of the little mind.*

'Sir, are you saying that one must see the immensity, the highest, and that the very perception of that puts what is possible at quite a different level and dimension; whereas if one holds on to the small possibility, the result in itself is small? Is this what you are saying?'

Yes, perhaps. More or less.

'I think I have caught a glimpse of it. I think I see what you mean by the impossible and the possibility of the impossible. But to continue with what I was asking, here I am with my vast conditioning, not only particularly but horizontally. I am conditioned by words; everything I do or think is the result of my conditioning. I see the necessity of radical mutation breaking through this conditioning. And you say that it is not a matter of time at all, that the very seeing is the doing. The very seeing brings about its own action. Again you said when you see a danger you act instantly. But we don't see the danger, the real danger of this conditioning. We don't see it, we don't hear it, we don't feel it. We have become so accustomed to it that we have lost all sensitivity to it. I think this is fairly clear—though I mustn't say "I think" because that again is a postponement of the realisation or the factual understanding of this conditioning.

'You said what seemed to me a most extraordinary thing, that the brain cells themselves, being conditioned for centuries and centuries can be made new. How is this possible? Is it really possible? I am using the word *possible* casually, quickly, to convey what I mean. Is it really within my capacity to uncondition the whole nature of the brain that has been shaped, guided, held by its conditioning?'

Not from what others have said or written, but as one observes one's own brain activity in daily life, the brain needs complete security. Any form of uncertainty or disturbance brings about confusion within it. Its constant demand is that it shall be completely, wholly, secure, safe, protected, not only from outside disturbances and accidents but also inwardly not to have any problems, not to have any form of disturbance such as quarrels and anxiety, guilt and so on. Through all these disturbances and anxieties it is always seeking to establish a great sense of security for itself. This security is denied when there is a division—a psychological division as well as factual division—as nationalities, as this and that, division after division, separation upon separation. All these factors bring a sense of chaos, a sense of confusion and conflict. And therefore it has to protect itself, to resist, and out of that there is fear and identification with something—with a belief, with an ideal, with a particular pattern of activity or with a nation—which again gives it a certain sense of security.

So the brain is always demanding, consciously or unconsciously, deep down or superficially, that it must be completely, wholly, at all times secure. And when it is not, it becomes neurotic and it finds security in neuroticism. But security—in the sense of complete protection, complete sense of being whole, healthy—can take place only when there is complete freedom—freedom from fear, freedom from anxiety, freedom from all the influences, from the propaganda, from the intrusion of the minds and words of people that are thoughtless, from the authority of the scriptures, of any propaganda or system. Freedom means freedom; not from *anything but* freedom. *When there is no prison the mind is free. It is only that kind of freedom that can bring security.*

The sense of complete freedom is not to do what one likes. To do what one likes is a reaction, the response of one's conditioning, and in that there is no freedom at all. But there is the quality of freedom in which there is security, a complete state in which the brain can never be hurt and can observe—without the implication of virtue. When there is freedom and the sense of security the very brain cells themselves undergo a radical change because there is the necessary atmosphere, environment for security and freedom to live together. This is really the total unconditioning of man, not only at the superficial level but at the very centre of his being; not only at the conscious everyday level but the deep, hidden recesses of his mind.

This can come only when there is no fear or the pursuit of pleasure. Then we will see that there is quite a different dimension and that there is great joy, an ecstasy which can never be destroyed.

29

INTENSE WATCHFULNESS

That morning the milkman told him that a tiger had killed a cow in the village and asked if he would like to go in the evening and perhaps see the tiger. He said they could arrange it by building a platform on one of the trees and tying a goat to the tree. To see a tiger kill a goat for one's pleasure was rather cruel and so nothing was done.

In those mountainous valleys it was cool and fresh. The dust had been laid by the recent rain and there was a sparkle in the air. The distant range of high mountains with enormous peaks was an extraordinary sight. As the day went by, clouds formed on those mountains and by the afternoon you couldn't see them anymore.

We thought that we would wander through the forest and perhaps come upon the tiger and see him at fairly close quarters. The cook said, 'Sir, you shouldn't go alone, and if you do, be careful.' We took his warning to heart and went out, down the path past the small village. Its saint was sitting with a few of his devotees around him, close to a temple with a thatched roof. As we passed he asked us to come and talk to him. But the tiger was more important, so we excused ourselves and went on.

The forest was now getting quite dense and as we crossed another path there was a snake, long, fat and looking dangerous. It lay across the path and it must have been over six feet, its black tongue coming in and out and its unlidded eyes staring. One had to go by that path to get deeper into the jungle so we waited. Presently the almost black snake made its way across the path into a bush and you could see it disappear. Then the path climbed steeply amid pines, deodars and heavy bushes.

The sun was just disappearing over the hill when we came to a little clearing. Suddenly there was a strange silence; the birds and even the trees seemed to hold their breath. Everything was motionless, there wasn't a stir, and one became aware that there was some kind of danger or a peculiar feeling of intense watchfulness. It is remarkable how the body acts at that moment. It quickly moved to the trunk of a tree and stood stock still. It was not the mind directing the body; the body itself acted on its own, independently, with assurance and without fear. The silence, that strange silence of danger, continued for some minutes and we thought we would see a tiger passing by, or some other wild animal equally dangerous. Suddenly a bird began to sing and the whole movement of the forest began again.

Apparently the danger had passed, but yet one felt it was very close by. We wanted to go on but the body refused. And since the body was more intelligent at that moment than the desire to see the tiger or the danger, it won. We remained there for some time, watching the light of the evening on the treetops, the beauty of the leaves, and the complete silence of a forest that was full of life. You could almost smell the sense of danger but it began to fade away.

We turned back, went down the steep path and came upon a horde of monkeys, black faced, grey haired, long tailed, almost as big as a man. There must have been over a hundred in all the surrounding trees, silently watching you—the babies, their mothers, the old gentlemen, sitting very quietly, almost motionless, watching you and wondering what you were going to do. The nearest one was extraordinarily intense, watchful. We had been told they might attack us but they did nothing of the kind.

They were as surprised as we were and the surprise and the apprehension disappeared as all of us were watching each other quietly without any fear. We moved and when we took a step down the path they all scurried away with a lot of noise and chattering. It had been for them a long pause in their activity, for it must have been at least two or three minutes. We had seen the monkeys but not the tiger.

Returning, we passed the temple and the saint in his shelter. Now there was a lamp burning and he was sitting alone, quietly, probably meditating, for you heard his chanting. The sun now was upon the distant peaks with a roseate glow, and as we went to the cabin there was that extraordinary feeling that comes of an evening when the sun is about to set.

The dining room, the sitting room and the bedroom were one. The cook had lit a fire and the flickering flames cast many shadows on the wall. It was not late. You found you were meditating. To make up one's mind to meditate so as to reach a certain state, to probe into depths that you had discovered, is to end all meditation. The will to meditate, to explore, that very will projects its own image. The shadow of that image is the experience that the mind gropes after. To take any posture, to *make* the body sit still, any effort to control, all these deny the swift movement of meditation. The dancing flames had a thousand voices.

PART TWO

EXPLORATIONS INTO LEARNING

30

EDUCATION IS TO BRING ABOUT THE EXTRAORDINARY BEAUTY OF ORDER

They were on the roof, on the veranda and on the trees, a whole group of them. They must have arrived late in the evening last night. Their little hands were picking at everything. They were in the big tamarind tree, pulling bunches of the fruit, tasting it, never finishing it and throwing it away. They were brown monkeys, long-tailed small animals full of restlessness, mischief, endlessly running to and fro. They were never still, scratching themselves, pulling their hair or cleaning somebody else's forehead and body. They would pick out little insects from the other monkeys and swallow them. Even though one or two were asleep, tired out, they were doing something with their hands. They made an awful mess of the garden; really very destructive animals but nobody seemed to mind them.

They were sacred and you must not touch or harm them. You could only catch them in big traps without hurting them, and take them far away. But pretty soon they were back, perhaps not the same but another group.

If you watched very quietly they pretended not to see you, but they were keeping a quiet eye on you all the same. There was a big male most of them were afraid of, carefully going around him, avoiding him. But when he left a tree they would trot after him. Perhaps he was the leader. They had exquisite hands, delicate, rough, well shaped and long. They appeared to be very intelligent. Later on in the evening as the sun went down they would be screeching in the big banyan tree. That tree was splendid, magnificent in its structure. It spread out its arms to welcome you. When children staged a play or a dance under the banyan the monkeys would complain. They were disturbed by the light, the music and by so many people. The gardeners and others would try to chase them away and in their own good time they would leave. They didn't like open spaces. Beyond the wide field there were fruit trees—chikoos, papayas, oranges, avocados and grapes—but strangely the monkeys never went there. What a good time they could have had there.

They never let you get too close to them. The big male would allow you to come within about ten feet; we would look at each other and pretty soon he would get bored. There was no fear in him but he kept a very alert eye, sharp and cautious. There were babies that clung to their mothers, and young monkeys with long tails, playing together, twisting in and out of the branches, but they never came near the big male. They scrupulously avoided him.

The next day the monkeys disappeared; not one of them remained. They must have gone over the hills to torture other trees and lay waste to the ground nuts. Sometimes you would meet them on the road. It was quiet now without them. The trees, bushes and little plants seemed glad they had gone. Even the birds didn't like them, especially the crows. Whenever a crow approached, the monkeys would scamper away.

It was rather fresh and cool that morning and the blue sky was very clear. The hills looked as if they had been sculptured by hands. A long line of bullock carts laden with hay was coming into the valley. In the room there were many teachers from different parts of the world. There was a tape recorder. The veranda was full of the scent of the jasmine.

'What do you think of these new teaching machines? They are in use in America. Children learn from the machine by themselves while the teacher supervises them. The children seem to learn much quicker.'

It is strange how everything is being mechanised. This

mechanical learning helps to make the mind more mechanical. You can't discuss with a machine. You may question it and it will reply but this may make more mechanical a mind that is already that way. Don't you think, sirs, that a child, a student needs a direct human relationship, not a machine? A teacher who cares, who is not merely giving information but who is a human being talking over the many things of life and its problems, may through the discussion make contact with a student and help to bring about a total intelligence instead of only fragmentary knowledge about a particular subject—however necessary knowledge may be.

'There is so much student revolt throughout the world. They seem to have no positive purpose. Their purpose appears small, destructive and violent, without any kind of discipline or consideration for human life. They think that by destroying they will create a new society, but history has taught us that physical revolution only brings tyrannies of different kinds. They don't seem to see this. They want immediate change, immediate results, and violence is their tool. I can understand this but I am horrified by it, for violence can only breed more violence.

'But apart from all this, as a teacher I would like very much to talk over with you and the others the question of discipline. The discipline of punishment and reward is still there, perhaps a little more subtly. Examinations may not be necessary—there are schools that are discarding them as a final test of capacity—but keeping a report of their studies is still a form of reward and punishment. We have, as you say, been conditioned by the promise of this and the threat of that. Our social and moral structure is based on that, and according to it various forms of discipline have come into being, religious and cultural. In this permissive society most of that is gone. If you ask a student what discipline means I am sure they wouldn't know. Or they would reject it altogether and say, "You have disciplined yourself and see what you have become.

Your order is chaos; your discipline has brought about wars and social injustice. We don't want that, we want a different society, and what you say about discipline and order has little meaning for us." But apart from what the young people say, one must have discipline. You can't do anything without it. If you want to paint your house you must begin in an orderly manner; you can't splash paint all over the place.'

What does that word discipline *mean? Doesn't it mean the act of learning, learning from a teacher, learning from the whole movement of life, of which one is a part? To learn there must be attention, and attention is order; not that you impose order in order to be attentive but the very act of learning demands attention. It doesn't matter what the subject is, whether it is painting or writing a letter, everything demands attention if you are to do it properly. We impose discipline on the student in the hope that he will learn how to concentrate on the book in front of him which doesn't really interest him. He wants to look out of the window at the hills or the breeze stirring the leaves. He is bored with what you are saying. You see him looking out of the window and you tell him to concentrate on the book or on what you are saying. He knows that if he doesn't he will somehow be punished, so he forces himself and makes an effort. That very effort makes him mechanical. Undoubtedly he will pass the examination but for the rest of his life he will be completely mechanical.*

When he comes rushing in from another class, ask him to sit quietly for a while. If he looks out of the window, ask him to look at the trees, the yellow leaves, the beauty of the hills, the colour of the poinsettia, the shadows, the villager. Let him look completely, without fear of not paying attention to the book or to what you are saying. Let his eyes rest on the beauty of the earth. When he has given attention to the things around him he can look at the book with the same attention, without any resistance. It is this resistance, in life as well as in school, that makes the mind unpliable, dull and afraid. From the beginning we drive children to be afraid and then reward them. The more sensitive a student the less he wants to be shaped by a system that is essentially based on reward and punishment with its disciplines and quarrels.

Order is necessary to do anything. One can discuss this, talk it over in a spirit of understanding and inquiry, communicating verbally without commands or threats, pointing out what disorder is, not what order is. The inquiry into the understanding of disorder brings about order, not the other way round. If you have a blueprint for order as dictatorships and, in a milder form, democracies have, anyone with any spirit will inevitably revolt against it. However, talking it over together with the student not only establishes a different relationship between teacher and student but the inquiry also helps the mind to be non-mechanistic. Such a mind uncovers the disorder of violence, of authority, of the standard morality—which is obviously immoral when you observe the absurdities of religious dogma which has caused so much confusion in the world, with its exclusiveness and so on. In the understanding of all this disorder, order comes about naturally. In this order there is no suppression, imitation or conformity.

So order is not something that is imposed by another, by you or society. It is a natural outcome of the daily observation of the disorder about us and in us. In the ordinary discipline of punishment, reward and conformity there is a great wastage of energy—through conflict, through suppression, through fear and through the pleasure of reward. This wastage seeks greater energy through violence, through the so-called freedom in which everyone does what they like, and through a constant pursuit of entertainment. So the few become very efficient and the vast majority of human beings just waste their energies and wither away. But when there is the investigation of disorder, and when out of that comes the natural mathematical precision of order, then there is the release of abundant energy, which will not become destructive, violent or mischievous. After all, this is the function of education, not to make the mind more mechanistic and thereby suppress the movement of energy which then becomes violent, brutal and full of all the ugliness that man has brought about. Education is to bring about the extraordinary beauty of order through learning about the dangers of disorder. Then the mind will lose all its aggressive, competitive, ruthless activity. The core of disorder is the self-centred activity which all societies and communities encourage in different forms. Having encouraged that, it ends up in violence and then society resorts to repression.

The teacher's profession is the highest. If he has not understood disorder in himself and in his surroundings, when he talks about order he becomes a hypocrite. The student smells hypocrisy very quickly. Therefore he has no respect for you or for anything else and pretty soon he himself becomes confused, disorderly, hypocritical. What you are, he becomes. Your society shapes him, conditions him to be violent, competitive or conforming.

The function of education is to show the student all this, not just one fragment of life. Without this, deep human care and affection is lost. Love is the very essence of order.

31

TEACH THROUGH DIALOGUE RATHER THAN MERELY IMPART KNOWLEDGE

We were very high up in the mountains; nearly seven thousand feet. From the window you could see the snow-capped peaks and in the early morning the highest was rose-coloured against that extraordinary blue sky. It would become as bright as a new moon, sharply clear. By mid-morning it would disappear; clouds and fog would cover it, but you would still see the lower mountains and the valley intensely blue, dark and mysterious. No wonder they worship the mountains. They say the gods lived there, the perfect ones, the great ones, from where they looked down towards the south, pouring out their blessing.

It would probably begin to rain in a few days, at least the local people said so, for there had been a rather dry spell. They warned that when the rains began, not to walk in the fields and over the hills for there would be snakes, and to be careful where one trod. People here were very poor and as you walked through the village you would see the filth of it. Nobody seemed to mind and they carried on with their daily lives adding more. Perhaps the rains would wash it away, but then the roads would be muddy and the paths covered over with water coming down from the hills. This would be welcome.

You walked in the woods, meeting many monkeys and an occasional deer, or you would see a big bear. They kept their distance. On the road one afternoon there were two boys, probably brothers, one a little taller than the other. They stood with their arms stretched out and their hands open, in torn rags, dirty, unkempt. They were begging, asking for money, and as we had no coins in our pocket we asked them to come to the hut where we were living and we fed them. One has rarely seen two children eat so much. Several cups of milk disappeared and quantities of rice and vegetables. You could see their tummies expand. Presently they had their fill and went away. Again in a few days there were those two boys on the road with arms outstretched and open hands, the blue sky above them. We asked them to come to eat but this time they shook their heads and with their thin fingers said no. Their mother had told them not to eat at the house of a Hindu for they were Muslims. They wanted only money and not the food cooked by another community. One almost had tears. They will remain hungry and the slow corruption of time and tradition is going to destroy them and others.

The rains came and went and the road through the village was muddy. The two boys and a little girl were standing in the same place as before and as one passed by they looked the other way. They didn't want money, let alone food. You stopped and talked to them but they wouldn't reply. There was no smile on their faces; they were hard, almost strangely angry. Their parents were doing a thorough job and slowly the seed of hatred was being sown in them. From then on they would ever be separate, congealed in their own antagonisms, bitterness and anger.

A new family came with little children. The next morning in the bright clear sunlight a servant had the baby resting on her bare outstretched legs. The baby was face down and, talking to it, the servant had taken a little oil and was rubbing its back, bottom, legs and on its head. She must have been doing it for at least ten minutes. Then she turned the baby over and gently, smoothly rubbed its arms, chest and tummy. Every part of it was oiled and rubbed and cared for. Presently somebody brought buckets of hot and cold water. She washed the baby and used some sort of powder that washed away the oil and it never once cried. The baby was so small, probably about six months, and presently it was wrapped in a clean white cloth. The baby looked so happy, pleased, and it was carried inside. Every morning in the sunlight it was bathed in oil, talked to, cared for and every morning there was no crying. There was only that gurgling noise that babies make when they are happy. They were there for several weeks. The mother and the father would be playing cards with others, endlessly talking. You would see the baby in the mother's lap being petted, hugged and kissed, but the servant looked on and took it away when the parents had enough of it.

The pines were now washed clean, fresh, and the grass was bright blue-green.

'I would like this morning to really go into this problem of discipline. We need it in schools, in the classrooms, in the dormitories. On the playing fields discipline is observed for the students enjoy playing. There you don't have to tell them what to do except how to hold the cricket bat, the tennis racket or the hockey stick; they take to it so easily. But in the classroom it is a matter of threat, punishment, reward and encouragement. How can we, not only as teachers but as human beings, bring about a natural order in ourselves?'

Have you noticed that when children are very carefully looked after by their mothers, really cared for and loved, there is a relationship between them, a subtle wordless communication in which the child is completely happy? They know that they are secure, know that they are really cared for and loved. This care and love does not bring about in the child any form of the resistance from which arises violent expression when they grow up. When there is overpopulation, when both parents have to earn a livelihood, when the children are neglected or cared for by the community, a nurse or someone else, you can see a different expression in the children. They are already being disciplined in the orthodox sense of that word. They are already conforming, and the discipline that is a slow death has already begun.

That inexpressible relationship between the mother and the child, the warmth, the subtle contact through words, through caress, through tenderness, can never exist in a crèche or kindergarten. It is this quality of tenderness between the mother and the child that creates the climate in which the child grows and learns, because it trusts, because it has no fear. This learning is the essence of order. Discipline in the sense of control, suppression, imitation, conformity with its reward and punishment, makes for violence. The word discipline *itself means to learn, and not the enforcement it has come to mean. And as civilisation is becoming more and more industrialised, more expensive, both parents go out to earn and the child is neglected. If you are rich you hand it over to a nurse or send it off to public school to get rid of it as quickly as possible. And the boy or girl finds themselves in an impersonal world with little relationship, with others like themselves, bullied by the older ones. And because they need security they instinctively form groups and imitate the older children. They do not want to be different, so the slow death of conformity takes place. This is known by all dictators and by other governments. Then discipline in the sense of enforcement is necessary and the culture in which they are brought up naturally encourages them to be violent.*

Violence is the expression of insecurity. It is the language of the insecure. It is only the insecure that revolt, that create havoc in the world; it is only those who are insecure who bring war. The brain can only function harmoniously, easily, happily in security. When there is insecurity the mind is distorted, and thought which is seeking security tries to find it in division, in separation, as in nationalism, in belief, in dogma, in formulas. This very division is the denial of security. So thought seeking security breeds insecurity. From this flows all corruption, violence, ambition, competition. If we understand, as teachers and human beings, that infinite care and the tenderness of parents is necessary to the child and between the teacher and student, then there is order which is an expression of intelligence. Intelligence is this sensitivity, this infinite care by the parent, which cannot be given by the government or a trained bureaucrat.

The teacher was silent for a while and then said, 'I follow what you are saying, I see the logic of it, but how am I to establish this sensitive relationship with a group of students? I really don't know them and they don't know me. They come with antagonistic resistance, running from one class to another, dashing off to the playing field and finally to their homes. The classes are growing larger instead of smaller. I can't physically talk to every student or care for them. One hasn't in oneself the energy for all this. In limited time one has to teach so many subjects each term. They must have acquired certain subjects by the end of that term. There is constant pressure upon the students and teachers which brings about a great strain. Taking all this in, how am I, wanting a decent relation with the student, to bring this about? Knowing the difficulty of the student, his possibly broken home, that the parents are occupied with their own pleasures or worries, knowing there are gangs in the schools, knowing the students are reluctant to learn, knowing too that most of them are in revolt and that they think they know everything, what is one to do?'

This is a question that is asked all over the world and it requires a great deal of intelligence on the part of the educator to take into consideration the insecurity at home, the unconscious desire of the student to find security in a group of his own and to turn his back on society. The teacher knows the parents have rarely established this sensitive relationship with the child and knows too that he himself is seeking security in relationship and is confused and in misery. Knowing all this, not only verbally but actually experiencing it without running away from it, aware of the fullness of it, then when the students rush into the classroom, have them sit quietly for two or three minutes. Explain the necessity of it, that when the body is quiet there is a self-recollectedness which brings sensitivity. Then both teacher and student can share this quality and discuss its implications before beginning the normal study of that particular class.

Discuss and teach through dialogue rather than merely impart knowledge. The most important thing is to bring about sensitivity in the relationship between the teacher and the student. In this sensitivity the authoritarian spirit disappears and the honesty of understanding and care is felt by the student. Therefore they will listen and this very act of listening brings about its own order. It is this order, born of sensitivity and intelligence, that frees the mind of all resistance. Order is a movement in freedom and this movement comes when you understand the nature of disorder. Violence is disorder; you cannot bring about order through violence. So one has to understand very deeply the whole issue of human action and life.

32

TO LEARN COOPERATION IS PART OF EDUCATION

To an old Mughal garden with ancient tombs a man on a bicycle came every day at the same hour. He would lean his bicycle against a tree and with his back against the same tree, facing one of the tombs, he would sit on the dusty grass, cross-legged with a straight back and closed eyes. He would be very quiet, his body motionless, and would repeat some chant. The green parrots had their homes in the little crevices in the dome over the tombs. There must have been thousands of them and they were noisy in the evening coming back home. There were crows and mynah birds, all of them making much noise in that quiet garden, and the man with the bicycle would sit there. When one had walked for half an hour or more around the tombs, among the trees and in the walled rose garden, the lights would come on in the streets and he would still be there. He was probably a clerk; he was a poor man and wore a dirty coat. He would say that he was meditating or saying his prayers. He didn't expect anything from this world except perhaps a few rupees, but he came there every evening after office hours. He must have been looking forward to it through the day. Children played around him and neighbouring servants would sit further away on the lawn, playing cards. He never seemed to pay attention to all this. He was used to the beauty of the dome, its blue tiles, the arch and the smell of the jasmine. During that hour or more he never opened his eyes; he was completely withdrawn, motionless. Only his lips moved and presently they too would be still. He would call himself a religious man. He kept his bicycle very clean and polished.

Is meditation an escape from daily life, from the monotony and boredom of it? Is it a further form of pleasure, an expansion of one's craving? Is it a projection of one's own desires contrary to one's own despair? Is it self-hypnosis, a vision of one's own conclusion, a longing symbolised in an image of the mind or of the hand? Is it an enchanting vision that one has conjured up from the past? Is it a conflict to hold wandering thought? Or is it an effortless deep quietness where thought has no place, though thought can function from it? Is it a silence which has no measure, neither height nor depth, a silence in which there is no centre as the thinker, the experiencer? It is a silence that can never be a result of control, of imitation, of effort.

Would the man with the bicycle understand all this? He had a very simple mind; he didn't want any of the complexities and subtleties of meditation. He had found a way of sitting quietly and repeating words that gave him tremendous satisfaction, a comfort he couldn't find in life. He wouldn't call it an escape, for it was very real to him. But the highly educated mind which has read so much about meditation, practised this method and that, been self-denying, acted according to a principle, such a mind wants something more than to sit under a tree or in a darkened room concentrating, hoping to catch a glimpse of something that will equally be satisfying and give meaning to life. All this is a form of entertainment and has nothing to do with meditation. There is an ecstasy which is not the effect of a cause, for in meditation there is no wastage of energy. Meditation is the summation of all energy which explodes into nothingness. Man is frightened of not being or not becoming. He must have a goal, a purpose, an end in view, and the supreme nothingness seems a denial of life. The understanding of the movement of all thought and action, which is living, is the movement of nothingness of meditation.

Now the parrots were quiet and the trees were filled with crows, mynahs and smaller birds. The man with the bicycle was totally unaware of the quiet of the evening, the loveliness of the dome and the beauty of the arch. Presently he got up on his bicycle and went his way.

'If I could, I would like to teach how to cooperate. That seems to me one of the major issues in learning. Though I have tried often, I really don't know how to bring this about. It seems to be the key to relationship. If it is not learned then discipline and enforcement become necessary, which in turn bring about what is happening in the world, this revolt against or blind acceptance of tradition. So this morning could we talk about that?'

What would you consider the most important thing in cooperation? Is it the object around which we cooperate, the people with whom we cooperate, or is it the intense feeling of cooperation, of working together, doing things together? Can there be cooperation around a belief, around an authority which represents that belief? Can there be cooperation, the spirit of it, the feeling of it, the depth of it, if there is any personal feeling involved, any personal profit or the fear of not belonging? If there is any of this, inevitably there must be division with contradictions and conflict. Life demands that we all work together. It is part of civilisation that we cannot possibly exist without the help of others. The more you are educated, in the right sense of the word, the greater the necessity of cooperation.

Working together does not mean thinking compulsively together, being subservient to the deeper or wider thought of another. When there is any feeling of subservience the slow poison of authority comes in. Authority can compel us to cooperate for our personal benefit or for a promise in the future, but intelligence is not the child of thought. Thought has its own barren children. When thought cooperates it must inevitably breed division and conflict. Thought is old but intelligence has no age. In cooperation there is no suppression or subservience.

'Isn't all this too difficult to convey to a student?'

For the moment we are not concerned with the student. We are concerned with whether you have the quality of cooperation as a teacher, as a human being. If I may point out, to you cooperation is an idea and you want to transmit it to the student, who will either reject or accept the idea. The description of that idea is not the actual fact of cooperating. We indulge in explanations and apparently they seem to satisfy. The description of a long cool drink to a thirsty man has no value at all. He wants water. So it must be found out if you as a teacher, as a human being, have really and truly this feeling of cooperation, of working together. Then the honesty of this feeling can be conveyed—it conveys itself. Without it, to talk about cooperation brings a hypocritical superficiality that is not cooperation. Without it, any civilisation will disintegrate. You may work together for a personal motive or goal, for prestige or for some national achievement; this is what is happening in the world and so society becomes corrupt.

Our question really is whether you as a teacher and a human being can be in love, not with the idea of cooperation but with the fact of cooperation. Then through talking this matter over with the students, through discussion you will convey it and they will feel your care, your intelligence and the deep urgency of it. When we really understand what it is to cooperate we will also know when not to cooperate. This is part of education. But the immature mind is always willing not to cooperate, to be in revolt; it is far easier than to learn what the truth of cooperation is.

'As teachers we haven't time. We are exhausted. We have so much to do both at home and in the school. What you are saying seems so true but yet...'

Do you really think it is a matter of time or lack of energy? Cooperation must be one of the main concerns of any human being, because this is far more important than any book or any subject for it involves the whole of living, in the present and in the future, not only for the student but for oneself. The teacher is a human being and if you haven't time to look at the sky you are not living. Because we have divided life into various professions and ourselves into various contradictions we say we haven't the time. It is because we are occupied with one fragment.

33

THOUGHT DIVIDES

There is a path that winds among the potato fields and the winter wheat, and further along there is a wide patch of green peas with white flowers. One passed tamarind trees and a mango grove. There were green parrots and vultures sat on the tallest tree. You went past ancient villages with temples so old they seemed to have no age. In the wheat fields there was a huge bull with an enormous hump. It seemed so harmless. You walked past and a few boys came and chased it to another field where it was again chased. But the bull never turned on them. You would often see it lying in the shade of a tree, dozing, chewing its cud meditatively.

There were many sannyasis on the dusty path, old monks with their begging bowls and worn-out sandals. The villages here were filthy and old men sat in the sun among the goats, dogs and cattle. Along this path thousands upon thousands of pilgrims passed to the river. On the road leading away from it, villagers went every day to the big city where they would sell their products for coins, a little oil, some cloth or a new bicycle pump. They would chatter going to the city but on the way home they walked silently back to their villages, crossing the rickety bridge and going up the little slope and beyond. What a beautiful country it is and how filthy and degrading are the towns. The river passes through them all, silently, sullied by them but cleaning itself as it goes along. It seemed never to be hurt, polluted. That morning it was there with its peace in the golden light of the sun.

We were sitting in a room that overlooked the river. There was a blue sky where the vultures circled higher and higher. On the veranda two pigeons were building their nest. It wasn't too cold that morning and one felt a great sense of peace. There were about thirty boys and girls sitting on the floor, all rather shy but wanting to ask a great many questions. One of them at last took courage and spoke, 'Why should I believe in God? All our parents and the people around us believe and we too must believe, but why should one?'

A girl, cleanly washed, fresh, with an open face said, 'I am really not interested in God. I don't know why you want to talk about it. I am concerned with my life, how to live rightly. Talking about God seems irrelevant. It may be necessary for the older generation but it doesn't affect my life. It seems utterly useless to talk about it.'

Are you not interested in why millions and millions of human beings are interested in God?

The girl replied, 'Probably I will be interested when I grow older but not now. I want to understand life and how to live. What has God to do with that?'

You know, human beings suffer a great deal. Their life is a great misery. They are always in conflict. Things come and go; there is so much uncertainty and human beings throughout the ages have wanted to know if there is something permanent. They say life is impermanent, a thing that passes away, and they want to find or believe in something that doesn't perish, that is permanent, that isn't made corrupt by the human touch. Not knowing if there is or is not, they believe, hoping with their hearts that something of that kind exists. For thousands of years human beings have believed, and killed each other for their beliefs. Except for one or two religions, they have fought religious wars.

When you say you are not interested in it, why aren't you? It is part of human existence. You may not believe in God but you may believe in a principle, in the perfect state, in a heaven or in paradise. It is all the same thing. Surely you must be interested in all the human endeavour. You may not be interested in mathematics but it is part of your education. In the same way you must be tremendously interested in everything that touches the human mind, its sorrows, its confusions, its absurdities, its belief in God or no belief in God. You must also be concerned with living, love and death, because all this is part of existence. So please do pay attention to what that boy asked. He asked why one should believe in God. It is a natural question because everyone around him and you believes in God. It is part of your tradition, your upbringing, as it is also part of the upbringing in those countries where they are instructed not to believe in God. So let us find out why human beings want to believe in something which they project out of their own suffering, uncertainty and confusion. Don't you want some kind of security, something to cling to, something that might protect you?

The boys and girls looked at each other seriously and with uncertainty. They didn't know what to reply.

Not only the few, but all human beings on earth must have security, food, clothes and shelter. Without physical security there is the fear of tomorrow. When there is fear our minds don't work properly, sanely. But as things are now, with one country against another, there is great physical insecurity. And so, wanting security, physical safety, we hold on to our little houses, to our patch of land, to our family, to our jobs. Also we want deep inward security; to feel safe, undisturbed, though we know that there is death, that there is pain, that life is a constant struggle with great loneliness. So we say to ourselves, not deliberately, that there must be something which is imperishable, absolute, and we believe in that. It is generally opposite to that which we are. So we say that God is love, everlasting beauty, peace, and this we transmit from generation to generation. We say we are Jews, Hindus, Muslims, Christians. This division with its supposed security divides people and so brings about insecurity, wars and hatred. This is clear isn't it? You see all around you one group of people against another group, one person against another. Your belief separates you from those who don't believe as you do. You may talk about loving your neighbour but beneath those words you are separating yourself by your belief, by your tradition and that peculiar arrogance that comes with the certainty of your own particular belief. So you see why we want to believe. For that belief we are willing to destroy each other. All religions talk about love and being kind to one another but belief itself destroys goodness, love and deep kindliness.

'I see what you say, sir. But why is there this desire for one's own safety, which takes the form of belief?'

As we said, physically we cannot function sanely if we haven't security, which is order, about us. That is the primary demand in all animals and in us too. It is absolutely necessary that all of us, not just the well-to-do few, have the basic physical necessities of life. This is not possible if you divide yourselves into Hindus, Muslims or some other category. That means you cease to call yourself Hindu, Muslim or anything else. Don't give yourselves labels. We are human beings not labels. Will you stop calling yourselves this or that? Otherwise you are going to create greater misery for man. This is part of your education; it is not just studying subjects.

One of the boys said, 'I may stop calling myself a Muslim but what about the people around me? My parents will be horrified and very angry with me.'

Then will you yield to them, go back to the fold that calls itself Muslim? As you have to learn mathematics, so you have to learn to deal with your parents when they get angry with you for not believing as they do. You have to learn about relationship, not just be told how to behave. Is all this too difficult? If it is, take a little bit of it, learn something out of it and go on learning. Don't just say your parents will get angry and therefore you must give in to them. Learn to live with them without having to believe as they do. It is no good just revolting against them, creating for yourself a little island, thinking that you can live by yourself or by joining others who revolt—then they will create their island in opposition to other islands. This again brings separation, antagonism, war. This has been the history of man. We must live at peace with each other and therefore we must understand how this belief which divides comes about. Deep down, inwardly, we are frightened, and not being able to resolve it we project an image of what we call God. We have created it. We create God in our image and to that we cling desperately because we suffer, because we are at war with each other and in ourselves, and because life is so uncertain. And ultimately there is always death. So we cling to the image we have made, the symbol, the thing made by the hand or by the mind. What is important is not what you believe in but why you believe; and if you go into it deeply you are bound to find that we all want a great sense of inward security. We all want inward peace and a feeling of deep, quiet, imperishable clarity. So thought invents various formulas, images and speculative hopes. Thought divides itself as the permanent and the impermanent. Being in itself impermanent it invents a permanence. Thought divides the world into nationalities, into groups, into individuals opposed to the community, and so on, endlessly. This division goes on both outwardly and inwardly. It is a kind of game played with ourselves and this game leads to great horrors, brutality and violence.

So you see how thought breeds hatred and arrogance, and you see how thought creates the image of what it calls God and love. These opposites are the product of thought and in this human beings are caught endlessly. All this has nothing to do with love, has it? You know what we mean by that word? To be kind, to be gentle; love has no fear; love is not jealous. Love is not a thing of thought. A thing of thought has in it a duality, one opposing another, but as love is not put together by thought, it has no opposite. This is a great thing to understand. Spend some time, as you do with geography, observing all this. Learn about it as you would learn cricket. Then you will see for yourself that any form of belief becomes totally unnecessary and you can live without any formula.

34

THE INTELLECT CAN NEVER BE FREE

A blackbird came every morning to sit on the tallest chimney, sing and supervise the rooftops and antennae. It was spring and the chestnuts were just beginning their tender green leaves. In that city spring seemed to have a special meaning. There was a peculiar joy in the air and the park was bursting with life. Every tree and bush was putting out new leaves and there were buds of flowers and the smell of spring. It was quite warm for that time of the year and as you walked among the trees and the promise of flowers to come you could feel the earth happy to be free of winter. There were daffodils and primroses and in the windows mimosa from the south. People went by with smiling faces. The sad ones were those returning from the racecourse who seemed glum, unhappy that their horse had not won. Children played with hoops, shouted and called to each other. The blackbird would come every morning, sit on the same chimney, sing and look over the roofs and the passers-by.

Just beneath the window was the single chestnut tree. It was not very healthy; many branches were sawed off. It had been trimmed too much to fit into the little garden and now in the early spring the new leaves were drooping. Before we left there were a few blossoms like candles among the green leaves. The river was close by and some of its bridges were very beautiful. The sky on that particular morning was extraordinarily blue, clear, soft and gentle. You could almost hold it in your hand, smell it, cherish it.

The shopkeepers of course had no time to look at all this nor had those who went to the races. There was an artist painting but he was so absorbed he failed to notice the little boy who came rushing to see what he was doing. Not being spoken to, the child soon left. The restaurants were full and the wide avenues were alive with people and cars. The huge flag under the arch, long and wide, made slow patterns of movement, graceful, welcoming. The man who had thought of putting that vast flag there must have thoroughly enjoyed seeing it. He was probably some kind of official and it must have lifted his life beyond the usual routine. Maybe he looked at it and walked away smiling to himself.

In the little room with its stuffy furniture were people of several nationalities. They had come to talk about education, their children and the general state of the world. There were tulips on the table. We were all rather shy; it was difficult to begin but after we had talked about the weather and the lovely spring, the green grass and the noise of the city, one of them said, 'I send my children to a private school. I like to see them and play with them when they return home for their holidays, but unfortunately one hasn't enough time or perhaps the inclination to watch over them. The private school system, if one can afford it, is better for them. Of course it is a system that emphasises class, the school tie and inevitable office. I am sure we all are aware of what is happening in other parts of the world where students are in revolt. Even in my own country this is going on. We don't seem to be able to offer them anything and as you walk down the principal streets you meet such varieties of long-haired boys and girls, unkempt and wandering endlessly. At least the intellectuals had a certain integrity, a certain way of looking at life—tolerant, somewhat cynical, self-contained and a bit aloof. But an aristocracy of intellect seems to be fading fast; it means nothing to the modern generation. They have no restraint; they do what they like, carelessly, indifferently, without any dignity. Intellectual striving with rigorous discipline has no place with this generation. There was in my country a certain continuity of tradition and a purposive aim. Now we are all becoming middle class. Even the so-called aristocracy are becoming vulgar. One feels a slow despairing disintegration.

'We watch all this without being able to do anything about it. We see the young going in hordes to listen to their kind of music and spend a few nights in tents in the open. It is squalid and uncomfortable yet they seem to be extraordinarily happy together. One has a feeling now that there are no wars and no absurd discourses of high prelates, that the young people and the country as a whole seem to have no vision. They are content to be happy for the moment with instant pleasures, immediate urges and the vain pursuit of nothing. I suppose we are really to blame for this for I have often wondered what I have done in my life that has any meaning at all. I suppose we are all failures from a certain point of view and in our folly we bring about our own destruction.'

Another responded, 'I don't know about that. In my country we still respect the intellect. We have created a marvellous structure of words; we still have great artists and writers. We adore taste in everything and we have led the world in that. We had our student revolt but it was contained. The exuberance of youth takes different forms; today it is revolt. But for us a good life is the main thing, appreciation of fine things—good food, good architecture, good music, and women of course. We have been satisfied with this and we have kept religion in its proper place. Though there were once wars about it, that was long ago.'

Yet another spoke, 'If you go through the country probably you would find people fairly satisfied, wanting to be left alone, completely self-centred with their little farms, pigs and chickens, taking their annual holidays. But in this country too there is a slow acceptance of decline. We are also becoming Americanised. Our education has been one of the best but it needs to be reformed. Fortunately the competitive spirit is not entirely wiped out, though it is nothing compared to what exists in the communist world. Competition there is deliberately cultivated and the best end up in Moscow. It is the same with their music, ballet, circus and in the scientific world. The world is becoming more and more ruthless and intellectual integrity is fast disappearing.'

How can you be honest if you are competitive? In competitiveness isn't there imitation and conformity to whatever society wants? Competitiveness is the very essence of conformity and society sustains those who conform, whether in the communist world or any other. The morality of competition is the corruption of society. There may be good taste in competition or vulgar aggression but as long as this spirit exists any society is corrupt.

'What would happen in a society where there was no competition at all?'

That is really an intellectual question put by one who is caught in competition, who therefore does not actually live in freedom from imitation and conformity. The intellect may imagine itself to be free from something but in reacting against competition it may fall into another trap in which competitiveness exists. The cultivation of the intellect is the result of time and therefore must be imitative, conforming. The intellect can never be free for thought is the response of the past which is the accumulation of the known. The known is ever creating the pattern of imitation; it is the spring of conformity and imitation.

'Are you against the intellect? Which means, are you for sentimentality, emotionalism and fancy?'

We are not against anything or for anything, but when one fragment called the intellect takes dominance over other fragments, as it does in most human beings, then there must inevitably be contradiction, conflict and confusion. When a people has laid emphasis on the idea, on reason, and worshipped that as good taste, the inevitable process of disintegration must take place. In that there is no harmonious growth or harmonious life and one feels this is the seed of sorrow and disintegration.

'Our education *is* the emphasis on the intellect. Without that intellect we would be mere savages. It is the intellect that has brought about this astonishing technology. It is the intellect that has developed vast industry, brought food and a better life to millions of people in underdeveloped countries. When the intellect is not functioning efficiently and reasonably there is physical misery. Intellect has brought about wars but it has also suppressed disease. One can see the vital import of the intellect. You are probably right when you say that to give emphasis to any fragment is to be dishonest and hypocritical in action, but that is how we have been brought up; we are heavily conditioned. As parents, whichever country we live in, whether we have the welfare state or a state that dominates the education of our children, we see this fragmentation of life. As you point out, giving extreme importance to one fragment must inevitably bring about disaster. I see this very clearly but as parents what can we do?'

'I suppose we can do quite a lot. I come from a part of the world where we are a happy race. We have blue skies, sunny seas and beautiful women but under the church we have been made to conform, to believe. Until recently our education was in the hands of religion and therefore backward. Now it is beginning to break up. The nuns are leaving, getting married, so are the priests. The old pattern is changing. But as you have said, it is superficial. I wonder if we really want anything very deep. A few of us may but the vast majority want comfort, good food and pleasure. We accept any education or government, whether tyranny or democracy, that guarantees us these. We will join together with other nations if this is guaranteed and we will create an educational system that will follow these lines. I personally want to enjoy life and when death comes I can't do anything about it. But pleasure is the main pursuit of man.'

Outside it was spring, the new. Love is always new. Pleasure is always the old. Love alone can bring about something totally new which the intellect can never understand. The intellect knows pleasure and the pursuit of pleasure but it will never know what love is.

35

KNOWLEDGE IS DETRIMENTAL TO LEARNING

The sun would not be up for some time. It was quite dark. The stars were extraordinarily bright, very close to the earth. The valley was utterly quiet. It had that quality of stillness that some ancient lands have, untouched by human beings, by their thoughts and their miseries, untouched by any passing civilisation, untouched by all the noise of towns and the cries of man.

At that time of the morning it is always strangely silent. One never feels this stillness in any other part of the world; it has a quality of penetration, very deep and full of space. The hills were dark against the starlit sky. As you looked out of the window there wasn't a thing stirring—no movement among the leaves, no dog barking, no jackals calling with their peculiar cries. In this still silence one was immediately aware of extraordinary space. Not the space contained in the valley surrounded by mountains—the silence in itself had the vast quality of space. It had no frontiers, no borders. It was there with the silence and thought could not hold it. During the late hours of the night before the sun rose there was this crystal clarity of silence with its immense space. And love was there—if it could be called that. All these were interwoven and seemed to spread over the valley and the hills, beyond the mountains to the seas. Occasionally during the day when you were walking by yourself without a thought, without a word, without any image, it was there among those ancient hills. You would feel it penetrate your very bones and it would go with you wherever you went.

That morning so early, clear and quiet, it was there, this interwoven movement, with great immediacy, persistent and embracing. You thought it came from one direction but suddenly you were aware that it came from everywhere, from those faraway hills, from those enormous rocks, the dry river beds and the deep wells, and so from your own heart. Every morning before the sun rose it was there, the love of it and the beauty of it. Then suddenly a dog would bark and the whole valley would awaken. The sun touched the hills and the great rocks. The bullock carts began passing with their rattling noise and the children were laughing. The day would pass and late in the evening this space of silence with its love would be there.

On that veranda overlooking the valley and the red blossoming tree was a group of teachers, educators, men and women from the north and south. We were sitting on a red carpet which went well with the flowers on the tree. As the sun was very bright, glaring, the curtains were drawn but there was enough light to see each other's faces.

A teacher asked, 'What is education? I know what the word means, but beyond the dictionary meaning over which we have so many interpretations, what does it really mean? You have been all over the world, speaking at many universities and schools; what do you think this word deeply means? What do human beings live for, what is it all about? If we don't know what this existence is about then our education has little meaning. It is only when we know the whole meaning of living that we can know its relation to education. To talk about education by itself, as we generally do, is mechanical and superficial. So if we are true educators we must find the relationship between the whole substance of living and education.'

Let us be clear that we are not discussing the purpose, the meaning or the goal of living. When you have a purpose or a goal it is an invention of the mind; an imaginative mind or a philosophical mind. When you have a purpose for living then the actual fact of living, the what is, *and the purpose of living become contradictory. In this division there is conflict.*

'But isn't all existence a movement in conflict, more or less?'

The danger of having a purpose is that it breeds or brings about fragmentation in our relationships. You have your purpose and another has his, depending on your conditioning and his, on your prejudice and his, and so on. We only ask if there is a purpose in life when we don't know how to live, when living itself has no longer any meaning. When living has become routine, mechanical, one invents or imagines a purpose that will always be satisfactory. It will always be something opposite to what actually is, whether it is God or the state or an ideological utopia. Living, the actual fact of living, is far more important than the purpose of living. The actual fact of living for most of us is a constant battle, struggle, pain, despair and all the travail of man. Isn't education to help humanity from childhood onward to be free of all this? Or is it only to be caught more and more in the trap, endlessly suffering, always in conflict, in competition, in violence? Surely education is concerned not only with gaining technological knowledge but also much more, with understanding and therefore going beyond the confusion and misery of man. As it is now, our education is concerned with one fragment of a person, one particular section, disregarding the rest. We are highly skilled in a particular direction and at the same time terribly dull and ignorant. So as educators, if I may ask, what concerns you?

'Obviously we are concerned with imparting information or knowledge about the superficial activities of man—geography, history, science and so on. We are mostly concerned with helping our students to gain information about a subject so that they can function as technicians which will give them livelihoods. I think this is generally what universities are trying to do, to make the students proficient in one direction so that they will have jobs. With the rest of life we are not concerned at all. The students may rebel against it but they will be caught in it because they have to work. As an educator I don't know how to educate my students or myself in the deep psychological sense.'

So the educator needs education. How is this to happen? You have your degrees and are proficient in certain ways but you are totally uneducated. Who is to educate you? Other teachers who are more proficient in their subjects? These super-educators are in exactly the same position as you; they are also wholly uneducated. Who is to teach you? Surely not books. These books are written by specialists who themselves are not totally educated, whether they are scientific or religious books. So the problem arises: from whom are you going to learn and is there anyone to teach you? Or have you to learn while teaching your subject; through the very teaching, through discussion, through dialogue learn how your own psyche as well as the student's is working? It is in this interrelation between yourself and the other that you begin to discover and therefore learn about the whole of humanity.

'Isn't it much easier to be taught than to go through the process of one's own discovery in which one may fail? Wouldn't it be better to be taught, to learn from another who is specialised in the structure and nature of man?'

When you learn from another, if that is at all possible, you do not learn about yourself; you learn what the other thinks. If you learn from another as you learn from a scientist, it becomes mechanical, it becomes merely knowledge, and knowledge is detrimental to learning. You can add to knowledge or take away from it but when you act from knowledge you are acting with the burden of the past. It is the very negation of action. Learning is not accumulating, as knowledge is. Learning and action are synonymous, they are not two separate things. Whereas acting from knowledge brings about a contradiction in the doing.

After all, that is what you are doing, are you not, sirs? You are giving knowledge to students, filling their brains with facts, theories and the knowledge that mankind has gathered in various fields. Having acquired knowledge they are going to apply it in action. This becomes mechanical. There are spurts of pushing forward but it is always mechanical. You want to do the same thing when you ask to be taught about yourself, about the whole of human existence. Your education is making the student mechanical, because you yourselves are mechanical with your specialised knowledge. To be mechanical is the easiest way of living, but the easy way is the most destructive and confusing way of life.

'I see this. I think I understand this very well. Aren't you saying that our minds have become mechanical and so is our way of living, and it's our education that has made us like this? And aren't you saying that when a machine learns about itself, it remains part of a machine? Are you asking us to break down this mechanical way of living?'

That is only a very small part of it. Learning is not mechanical. We are not talking of learning about *something, we are talking about the state of the mind that is learning—the quality and not the subject of learning. Learning about something is one thing and learning is another. Learning about something is acquiring knowledge. Knowledge is always accumulation and therefore the past. Learning is a movement. Learning is not in the past, it is always a movement in the present. Therefore a mind that is learning is always alive, fresh, vigorous, and the very learning brings its own decision. The word* decision *usually implies an act of will, but the decision that comes with learning is not born of will and therefore is non-dualistic.*

KNOWLEDGE IS STATIC

You never can tell when you wake up how far away you have been. In the quiet still morning you feel you have been so far away and so alone that the room, the trees and garden seem not to exist. The walls are there and the outlines of the tree and the small garden. There is a vast space about you but you are not of it. The outlines of the hill, the hoot of the owl and the quiet deep silence of the valley seem to be in a space which your mind has not made.

That morning when you woke, your body was completely relaxed with closed eyes. There had been no dreams at all and hardly a movement. As you came back from that far distance you saw your body lying there, curled up and still. The brain which had been so quiet for many hours was reluctant to wake up. It wasn't exactly lazy, but it didn't want to be active. It would soon be aware of the sunrise, the light on the hills, the bullock carts going by, the breeze among the leaves and the children shouting and playing. But now it wanted to remain completely quiet without any thought and without any reaction. It was completely empty of memory, of the things it had to do. This emptiness had a strange quality of beauty. It wasn't the beauty of the hills or of pictures or of music, or of any word. It wasn't a beauty that could be expressed, for expression has not the quality of this beauty of the mind that was strangely aware without any movement, without any centre.

It lay there for over an hour, awake but very still. The body didn't move and all movement of thought was absent. This quality of emptiness had the peculiar resonance of love because there was such vast space. How long this would last seemed to be of no importance; the length of time would come only when the movement of thought broke in. But thought was as far away as those mountains of snow. It would have crossed many miles before it came near. In the short interval of the night the brain seemed to have renewed itself. There would be the daily speech and the ever-limited activity of thought. But somehow what was to come had no importance. The blue sky would be there, the ancient hills and beyond the tamarinds the big banyan tree. It was to be a lovely morning, scented, fresh and clear, but all that didn't exist. *What was* was the vast emptiness with its beauty and love. And that was enough for all life.

'We are imparting knowledge and information that is mostly mechanical. We have acquired so much knowledge, especially in the last hundred years, about every subject I can think of. We are adding to it with such astounding rapidity that it is almost impossible to keep up with it. As a teacher I prefer to teach in schools rather than the university and I have often wondered what the place of knowledge is and what is its importance. I am not sure this vast knowledge is not destroying us. I have taken my doctorate but what is the good of it? When I discourse on a subject with pretentious importance, keeping a wide space between myself and the student, I often question the worth of this knowledge.

'The other day I met a friend from a village who has no degree, no pretentions of higher education but he had a smile on his face. He welcomed me with such warmth that I was embarrassed. I was from the town and he was from the hills. He was human and I had become mechanical. Knowledge seems to make us more inhuman, distant, fragmentary and deeply without value. Yet I am imparting my knowledge to my students, making them more mechanical and inhuman, more than my fathers were. It seems so infantile and yet I am caught in this trap. So could we all consider this?'

Knowledge is one thing and learning is another. One leads to bondage, the other to freedom. Freedom is never mechanical for it is not put together by thought which is mechanical. Freedom is not in the known; it is not an accumulation of the known. The accumulating of knowledge, as a squirrel accumulates nuts, has become the business of our life. The more we have of it the more we feel secure, important. The action of knowledge is mechanical, repetitive, and in this habitual repetition we feel safe, protected. We feel we cannot be hurt. It is a shield against doubts, fears and uncertainties, and within the enclosing walls of knowledge our life and the activities of the brain seem secure. You can impart knowledge but not the act of learning. Learning is never accumulative for learning implies an active movement in the present with its curiosity, its intensity, its eager pursuit. If the act of learning is tethered to the post of knowledge it can only learn within the radius of the thing to which it is tied. In this there is no freedom. It is like a prisoner whose freedom is within four walls. This prison is knowledge and so he is never free.

'But without knowledge there will be no action. In the system in which I was brought up knowledge is one of the paths to reality, as is devotion or action. There are four main paths. One person may belong to one path and someone else to another but knowledge is necessary, as action is necessary, as is this feeling, this passion, this longing for reality. You seem to be against knowledge and yet you talk about action. Perhaps you could go into this a little more.'

Action without knowledge is inaction. All life is action. Life demands knowledge. There must be knowledge about the universe around us, about the various activities of our life, knowledge of nature, of the past and so on. Without knowing where your home is you could not return there. Knowledge is absolutely necessary but action related to that knowledge must be mechanical. Caught up in a mechanical way of living we seek escapes which are not mechanical, like entertainments, religious performances or sexual pleasures. But all these too become mechanical and we see that action based on an organised idea, which is knowledge, can never be free and must inevitably collide with life with all its varieties of movements, and must bring about not only division but conflict. Knowledge is static, always within the field of the past. Life is a movement, ever changing. A man caught in the past, living in the past with all his thinking based on the past, will inevitably lead a life of conflict. So the question is: can this mind with its brain, which is the result of the past with all its knowledge and experience, be free to experience the new?

'But I'm not sure I want to discover the new. I want security and in the new there may be no security at all. Knowledge gives me security in my job, my profession, with my family and in all the relationships I have. I want security, a feeling of complete certainty. Anything new, the unknown, leaves me uncertain, fearful.'

To function properly sanely, objectively and therefore efficiently, the brain must have complete security. Does this security lie in knowledge, which is the past, or in the total understanding of security? We need security but we destroy that security through division, through fragmentation, through different races, classes, nationalities, the rich and the poor and so on. In this very division is insecurity. Though we start out wanting security we build a structure, social, economic and so on, which brings about total insecurity. Thought which has sought security in various fragments destroys what it is seeking. In non-fragmentation there is complete security. As an educator one of our major problems is not only to impart knowledge but to point out the enormous danger of it. In becoming aware of the danger of it there is an action that is not mechanical.

'As a grown man I see the subtlety of what you are saying and I also see the importance of it. But how can this be imparted to a student who is not interested, who dislikes study, who is impatient, who won't listen? The arrogance of youth is colossal; you can't penetrate it. He wants instant understanding of life, he wants to go to the heart of things immediately and change the whole universe instantly, according to his particular pattern of course. How is a teacher to break through all this and help him to learn?'

If a teacher is learning, and really means it, he can convey this honesty to the student, convey this sense of integrity. But if a teacher is using the word learning *to cover up his own obstinacy, his own lack of passion, then the student who is alert to hypocrisy will not listen at all. This fragmentation—the teacher and the student, the guru and the disciple—ceases when the teacher, the student, the guru and the disciple are learning, through discussion, through dialogue, through investigation. Truth does not lie in the dialectical process of opinion opposing opinion, prejudice against prejudice, but rather in trying to understand the whole movement of life.*

'But why does the mind become mechanical? Is there a way of living that doesn't soon become mechanical?'

Seeing is acting. In the immediate action of seeing, division doesn't exist. We live on conclusions and formulas of which we are totally unaware. Without becoming aware of these perception and seeing is not possible. Awareness without choice of our conditioning, seeing the danger of the conditioning, this very action is the ending of conditioning. When you see a physical danger there is immediate action. But we don't see the danger of a mechanical way of living with its false security and so we drift along with it, confused, fearful and in sorrow.

37

KNOWLEDGE BECOMES AN IMPEDIMENT TO RELATIONSHIP

We were flying very high on a clear morning. To the east the horizon was filled with mountains, range after range of snow-covered peaks. We were probably several hundred miles from them but they seemed very close and very clear. They looked like clouds, rose-tinted, and there was silence between them and us. Beyond miles of open space these fantastic peaks rose over twenty thousand feet. Far to the south there were clouds and for a moment you thought they were mountains too. It was really a marvellous morning, simple, clear. You could see the horizon to the west and vast plains. Where the earth and heavens met there were dark shadows and rivers.

They were drinking their morning coffee. No one bothered to look out the window, or they had seen it so often they were indifferent to it. They were more interested in their papers and in talking endlessly about nothing. In spite of all this chattering and the sound of the engines one felt extraordinarily peaceful. There were the mountains with their splendour and the sacred river winding its way far below.

Prayers are absurd. That river and those mountains never prayed. There they were, the marvellous mountains reaching up to the skies and the sparkling waters of the river in the morning light. The supplications of man for help and guidance are part of the ignorance that brings self-hypnosis and gives continuity to his sorrow. Some rewards may come but you will become a slave to them.

A lady was saying, 'I am coming to this country for the first time and I am going to the place where the Buddha preached his first sermon. I have become a Buddhist. There is far more to it than to Christianity; it appeals to a reason that no other religion I know of has touched. I am making a pilgrimage from the fog and cold of London and I am quite absorbed in all that the Enlightened One has said. It will be a sacred moment when I reach that place and I am happy that I can come.'

She had beads in her hand and was silently moving them with gentle fingers, eyes closed, and was absorbed in the Pali words. But throughout those several hours of flight she never looked at the mountains, at the river below, winding in and out of the villages and towns. She never saw the beauty of the land, of the sky or the walled villages. She was absorbed in what she had read and now was going on a pilgrimage. There was a great sadness about it all. And man had covered the earth with his sorrow.

In that room with its red carpet, with the scent of the jasmine and the stillness of a red flower, one of the teachers said, 'We talked yesterday about knowledge and how it creates the image of our being. Our minds have created so many images with their own data and these images pop up at every moment of life. Whenever there is a challenge these images immediately respond. Each image has its own peculiar knowledge, absorbing the new and rejecting some of the old. Apparently one can never look at anything without these images. After what you said I tried to look at a tree and at my friend. Instantly various images came up to meet the tree and the friend. This is knowledge after all, not only book knowledge but also knowledge from everyday contact.

'Each image is strung together with the fine movement of thought, like a wonderful pearl necklace. Thought has made the images and thought holds them together. To go beyond the known, beyond thought, is to hold thought in abeyance. This seems to me to be one of the most difficult and arduous things to do and to convey all this to a student who is just beginning life seems quite impossible. Yet I feel it is one of the most important things for a student to learn. I'm not just repeating this after you; I have spent many years in meditation and thinking about all these things. But somehow I become increasingly confused and the clarity with which I began to inquire is gone. My own life has become a hideous mess. How can this image business end? Not only the image about myself, which I show to the world, but the images that I have of others which exist with the background of thought.

'You see, sir, I approach a new student quite openly without any image, which is without any judgement, and as I look that boy or girl conveys to me their peculiarities, their shyness, their fears, prejudice and arrogance. I haven't any images of them, yet they inevitably project facts about themselves. What is it in my mind that receives these? When I look at them I just look with openness; and now the mind has received the facts about them and it is these facts that become the image. From that moment on I look at them with the thought of these facts. Thought records these facts and there is recognition in them. They are implanted by thought in my mind. What is the nature of a mind that can look at the facts a boy has shown about himself and yet remain without their imprint?

'Perhaps I can put it differently. The machinery of thought is in operation all the time. It receives various forms of stimuli which become knowledge. My whole life is in this movement of thought. Perception of any fact—that the boy is fifteen, long-haired—is a process of recognition and this takes place instantly. Therefore any action of my mind about the boy seems to me inevitably a process of thought. I'm sorry to have made such a long speech. I think my question is fairly simple, though I may express it in a clumsy way. The heap of knowledge which is thought is constantly playing its part in whatever I am doing. This is a fact both with the boy and with myself.'

The defensive and offensive mechanism is in operation in both the boy and the teacher, and knowledge becomes an impediment to relationship. Knowledge is not love. Yet the mind cannot operate without thought. Thought is its very substance. So what is the question?

'My question is: doesn't thought, through recognition, through identification, inevitably interpose itself in any relationship?'

Of course. Obviously. What is the question?

'You have said over and over that knowledge, which is thought, is the corrupting influence, that it prevents direct and unconditioned perception. I am saying that it seems to me that thought, knowledge and recognition are intrinsically part of the mind's action. Seeing almost anything activates some knowledge which then colours further perception.'

Are you asking if one can look at anything without the machinery of thought and still function in any way? You are really asking, aren't you, if one can be free of this mountain of knowledge which is thought? Freedom from thought is absolutely necessary in order to see what is new, what is truth. The mind is caught in the habit of thought and in this habit there is a great sense of comfort and security. When one really understands the dangers in this desire for security and comfort, intelligence can and does use knowledge without being caught in it. When you see that boy and recognise his projections of fear, shyness and so on, intelligence will operate while recognising the images. Intelligence is the understanding of knowledge and its dangers. Intelligence can use knowledge in instructing the boy, without the instructor himself being caught in the whole mountain of knowledge. Intelligence cannot misuse knowledge—that is the whole point— intelligence being sensitivity, care, love. It is the mind that has not seen the mechanism of thought, its recognition and accumulation, that uses knowledge mischievously, dangerously. Thought in the hands of a neurotic can bring about great havoc and the world is full of people with knowledge of science, politics and economics. Intelligence cannot be fragmented.

Fragmented thought is no longer intelligence.

'How can I convey all this to a group of students for whom I am responsible?'

You will convey it if this intelligence is in operation. Part of the education of both the teacher and the student is to learn what this intelligence is.

38

FREEDOM FROM THE KNOWN IS THE HIGHEST INTELLIGENCE

It had been raining for some hours that morning and after a few days the earth would be green, fresh and young again. The wells would be full and the streams would begin to murmur; the rice fields would turn green, the cattle would get fat and the earth would be rejoicing. It had not rained for many months and the earth was parched, cracked, hard. There was that smell of rain on a dry land which comes in the tropics, a sweet nostalgic smell. The rocks were glistening, washed clean again and the leaves had no dust on them. The villagers would be glad for there is little rain in these parts. When it comes they seem to get a little fat, their faces seem to fill out. They are a lean, dark people but they have strength to dance and make merry. You see them on festival days, the old and the young dancing wildly with great vigour, stamping their feet to the drum and flute, hair falling over their faces. Round and round they would go and the hills and the valley seemed to be filled with their merrymaking.

There was a dark hill with a curiously animal-shaped head, and over it would be the slip of the new moon in the western sky. You watched it grow bigger and bigger and on the night of full moon there was a strange quality of silence that filled the valley. You would see the dark, deep shadows and the silver of rocks. There would be great rejoicing though there was little to eat, and then the usual routine of village life, the boredom, the squalor and the great poverty, inward and outward.

One wonders what it is that holds that valley unspoiled with its tamarind and banyan trees, the mango and the banana.

It is as though man could never spoil it; it is remote, silent, as it was at the beginning. Of a night you would hear an owl hooting and from across the valley its mate or its friend would answer. You felt you would like to join them. You couldn't see them but during the night they would call to each other. And again there would be great silence, penetrating and timeless.

The same group of teachers was in the little room. There was a smell of jasmine and you could see its flowers just over the parapet wall and the red flowers of a tree. 'What is the function of a teacher, not only as a guru but as a teacher in the modern sense?'

A guru is one who points the way, points out the truth or the falseness of something, one who clarifies the way to truth, who helps to remove the burden. That word implies all this doesn't it? But generally the guru becomes the authority, asserting that he knows, that he has experienced, and imposing upon his disciple a particular system. So instead of lightening the burden he adds his own weight of a system. All this is implied in this word which has now been added to the English language. The teacher in the wide and narrow sense has the responsibility not only of transmitting information but also in the very giving of that information to see that students bring about in themselves that quality of mind that is highly sensitive and therefore supremely intelligent. The cultivation of this intelligence is surely the function of any teacher, whether he is a guru or the instructor of technology.

'What do you mean by intelligence? It seems that this is one of the most important things to understand. We have a great deal of knowledge gathered through centuries about the natural world, about mankind. Can't an abundance of knowledge bring about intelligence?'

Intelligence is one thing and knowledge is another. Knowledge is gathered through experience, through repetition. It is the accumulation which is tradition. Knowledge is always contained in the past. You can add to it or change it but it is a residue anchored in the past. From this past knowledge most activities spring. Without knowledge you cannot catch the bus or put together a computer. Knowledge is necessary.

Intelligence comes about only when there is freedom. Freedom is not to do or think whatever you like and express it or not. Freedom is not something to be taught or learned from a book. There is freedom when there is an understanding of conformity with its action of will and the decision of choice. There is no freedom when the mind is tethered to any form of belief or conclusion. Freedom cannot be when there is fear, when there is identification with something other than what is. *Freedom cannot possibly be when there is the observer and the observed, the thinker and the thought. Freedom is not a reaction, for all reactions are the continuity of conformity. Freedom is not when there is effort, the struggle between the opposites, which is an endless corridor. Freedom from the known is the highest form of intelligence. That intelligence can operate in the field of knowledge but it is always free of knowledge. Intelligence is a movement, sensitive, alive, active, ever awake and knowledge is not. It is the function of the teacher to bring about this intelligence in the student. This intelligence is not personal, it is not yours or mine. When it is yours or mine, or of the community, or of the few, it ceases to be intelligence.*

'I think perhaps I may intellectually understand this, but through what method am I to cultivate that intelligence in the student?'

An intellectual or verbal comprehension of what intelligence is, is not understanding at all. Understanding is a total not a fragmentary affair; you either understand or you don't understand. If one may point out, when you say that you understand intellectually you are looking at intelligence through a fragment which you call the intellect, and this very fragmentation is the denial of intelligence. Any fragmentary approach negates intelligence. Intelligence is not to be captured through technology, which is one of the many fragments of human life, nor can it be had through any other fragment. Intelligence is the perception of the whole, the total seeing which cannot be if the mind functions in fragments. If this is clear, not verbally but actually, as clear as that red flower on that tree, as clear as the danger of a cobra, then would you ask, 'How am I to bring about this intelligence in another, by what system, by what method'? The method, the system not only brings about a mechanical mind but also brings a division between the pattern and the one who practises the pattern. This is conformity and therefore denial of freedom, and so it cannot possibly bring about intelligence.

'Again I catch a glimpse of what you mean. I am beginning to see in myself the light of intelligence. How am I to bring this light to the student who comes with a background of conformity, with a fear of not passing examinations and therefore not finding a livelihood? The student, however much he may be in revolt, is a conforming individual. How am I to convey the beauty of this light to him?'

Surely you can convey this through any subject you are teaching, through discussion, through establishing a new relationship with the student, not as one superior and one inferior, the one who knows and the other who doesn't know, but a relationship in which there is equality, a sense of care, affection, love. Then discussion offers a means of conveying all this. You establish a different kind of communication with the student in which both the taught and the teacher are learning. Both are working together, creating together, living together. This establishes a completely different kind of relationship which will naturally bring about the quality of intelligence.

'Surely this cannot be done in a class of thirty students. Perhaps it can be done with a dozen but in the mill of today's education, passing one subject after another quickly day after day, it becomes an impossible task.'

Perhaps. But if the majority of teachers are concerned wholly with the cultivation of intelligence then would the numbers matter? Among thirty there would be ten, more or less, who would capture the same light. So what matters is that the teacher himself be intelligent in the sense we are using that word. Then that intelligence is in operation all the time, not only in the class but when you are eating together or walking or playing. It is like the wind among the trees. The wind is a single movement and there are a thousand leaves. If you as teachers really care profoundly then this intelligence will operate in its own way, not in the way you want it to operate. When you bring into it your particular desires or ambitions then such activity is a total denial of intelligence.

'But schools all over the world are based on results, the hierarchical structure of educational bureaucracy in which groups fight each other for position, prestige, each one seeking a safe corner within the system. How can this monstrous structure called education ever allow this intelligence to function? On the contrary, governments, societies, bureaucracies do not want this. They see a danger in it.'

This is so. Societies, communities and the cultures they have brought about are concerned only with conformity. Within the pattern of that conformity there may be sporadic revolts but they soon pass away leaving the pattern altered only a little here or there. All reformations need further reformation, which is endless. This is what you accept as inevitable, see as impossible to change, and so lose all energy and passion. But when you see for yourself, uninfluenced by another, and have this quality of intelligence, then it will operate. You will have the passion, the energy, the drive, seeing what is *and going beyond it. The seeing* what is *and going beyond it is intelligence. Intelligence is a total movement, like love. It is not fragmented. That which is whole has a peculiar way of working in darkness with its own light. It is not dependent, because it is a light to itself, which nothing can destroy.*

Unless you have this religious ardour, the mountain appears insurmountable. If you have it the mountain does not exist.

39

SEX BECOMES AN OBSESSIVE GOD

There was something very nice about starting out early in the morning. The sun would not be up for several hours and the city was quiet. Before the sun rose there would be music for it was the beginning of a festival. There would be singing, chanting and instruments would be played, and the inevitable noise of the radio. But now everything was quiet and the bridge across the river was empty. As you went towards the west you saw to your left the Southern Cross.

The headlights of the car picked out the road and against the starlit sky you saw the outline of palm trees, casuarina, tamarind and mangoes. It was too dark to see the dirt and squalor or the terrible poverty but you felt it was there. The stars were very close and brilliant. You went speedily on the empty road alongside a great sheet of water for it had rained quite heavily during that monsoon. There were no bullock carts or lorries yet, only the Southern Cross and the trees between the car and it.

Gradually the stars began to disappear and the few clouds became pink and rose in the early morning light. You began to enter the hilly region. There were monkeys, lazy, waiting for the sun to come up before looking for food. Now came the bullock carts, the lorries and the villagers, thin but strong, walking from one village to another. The land was extraordinarily beautiful. The dew was on the cactus and the banana leaf. There were rich green rice fields and white herons were everywhere. You passed village after village and the aching poverty was there. You felt it more because of the beauty of the land. The villagers were used to it; they couldn't do anything about it. They needed help and the promises of the government and officials were far away. You crossed a narrow bridge over a running stream as the car climbed a steep road into the ancient hills.

There was still dew but now it was getting hot. After following a winding road you came down into the valley. It was a forgotten land and all the bustle and noise of civilisation seemed never to have come near it. There were goats eating every green thing. There was water in the river bed and you saw the big banyan high over the other trees. There was a certain quality, which one rarely felt anywhere else, in the ancient hills, the hard earth, the quietness, the purity of the air and the vast stillness that seemed to cover the land.

'Can we talk this morning about something which may be a difficult and delicate subject? I do not know if the others are interested but I would like to talk about sex. It is not only a personal problem, but being teachers dealing with adolescent youth I feel very strongly that we must have a sane and clear understanding of this subject. Parents don't talk about this with their children, or if they do it is inhibited or a thing that makes them shy. Tradition has made sex into something that is an impediment to spiritual life. In the West, in a society that is permissive, it has become a casual affair. So this morning I would like very much to consider this question.'

As it is a very complex subject one must be free to examine it, free to learn through investigation. If there is any prejudice for or against, any kind of inhibition about it or a conclusion, investigation becomes impossible and learning comes to an end. This is rather difficult for most of us because each culture has its own particular conditioning about this matter. If we are to find the truth of it we must be aware of this conditioning and not let it interfere in observing what is.

There are several things involved. First, why is it that society has made sex into such an extraordinarily important thing? One then has to understand pleasure and beauty, the responses of the organism and the religious sanctions involved. If we take only one fragment and are not concerned with the rest we will never wholly understand the issue. Understanding is not intellectual or verbal, it is to see the whole implication of it, the subtleties, the contradictions and conflicts. In most of our lives there is hardly any sensitivity to beauty. You may see a beautiful picture, a marvellous ancient temple and the sculptured hills but never feel intensely or passionately the beauty of the earth and the sky. One wonders why.

'I live here and I have been to other parts of this country but somehow I have not noticed, except casually, the richness of the land, the trees or the flowing waters. My mind doesn't look at this. Now that you point it out I too wonder why I have not noticed these things. I have seen them through the window of a train or while sitting in the shade of a tree with a book but I have never been close to them. Nature is something that is there, but that is all. I could do a bit of gardening but I don't. Is it because I am so absorbed in myself, so occupied with my problems, the worry to make ends meet? Is it that I have closed my eyes to everything but my own urgencies?

'For some years I was a sannyasi. I turned away from the world to seek reality. Monks are not allowed to have any feeling for the beauty of the world; one sees the danger in it and shuts one's eyes not only to women but to all the movement of nature. Through association one may get entangled in lust and that is a tremendous barrier to reality. At least that is what tradition has taught us. But today monks are marrying, breaking their vows and so on. By nature we are traditionalists and beauty is a dangerous thing. During those years when I ate what was given to me, it was our custom never to taste separate food but to mix it all up. Any form of enjoyment was denied. We never even thought about beauty, we didn't dare. And now, although I have become a layman, all the past years of tradition are a part of me. I can look at those hills and the lovely children playing in the field but the beauty of colour really means very little to me.'

Another teacher said, 'I am very fond of literature, not only of this country but of the world. I read a great deal and I see the beauty of a poem, a style of writing or a well-constructed story. I can see the beauty in all that but I am not intimately in relation with nature. I am rather nervously apprehensive of it, if you know what I mean. I prefer to remain in my room with a book than go for a walk in the hills. I don't know what beauty means to me; probably it is only an intellectual concept.'

If there is no beauty with all its marvel in one's heart then action becomes very superficial. Your gods and your literature, the trees, the women, the men, are used for your own personal pleasure. Is love pleasure, desire? Without understanding this basically, sex becomes a problem. We never ask ourselves why civilisations, whether in the East or the West, have given to it such enormous meaning and importance both religiously and humanly. Pleasure becomes mechanical, as thought is mechanical—whatever it touches becomes routine, boring, or is used to sustain a particular form of pleasure. Pleasure is one thing and joy is another. Joy can never become mechanical. It happens and then thought, thinking about it, makes it into pleasure. It is the same with profound enjoyment; the moment thought captures it, it turns to envy.

If one does not really see this, how mechanical one's life has become with no freedom, one will use sex either for pleasure or as an escape from oneself, from the deadliness of our lives, from worries, anxieties, conflicts. There, at least for a few minutes, is a cessation of all this—through it or in it we hope to find something transcendental. Intellectually we are slaves; our energies are taken over by technological activities. We are bound and conditioned in the prison of the past and here at last we find a sort of freedom, an action in which for a moment one escapes from inhibition, fears, anxieties and guilt.

So sex has become an astonishingly vital and important thing. It is encouraged in certain cultures. In others it is discouraged but it goes on under the surface. In a permissive society it becomes promiscuous and therefore relationships become rather casual. There is the warmth of living together, feeling casually friendly, drifting from person to person or from one group to another. In all this one sees the activity of pleasure with its temporary satisfying comfort. There too there is no beauty. The casual tenderness is not love, and without love sex becomes an obsessive god.

To really understand this problem there must be the freedom that comes with understanding oneself. The religious denial of sex breeds deep inward conflict which is a great wastage of energy. Celibacy hopes to conserve this energy in the service of reality, God, the state, or what you will, but the real deep wastage is conflict. One totally disregards that. Beauty, freedom and love are not formulas or concepts invented by the intellect. When one lives by conclusions one is ever living in a world of conflict, struggle and pain. Sex is not a problem by itself; it is related to all existence. We try to solve one problem by itself as though it were separate and unrelated. To deny or to worship sex indicates a mind that is fragmented. In fragmentation there is no freedom but mechanical activity in which neither beauty nor love can be. Our real question is not of sex but whether one can see life as a total movement, not broken into various pieces. Then the seeing is the doing. It is not to see, form a conclusion and act according to that conclusion; this is fragmentation. We are unaware of this in ourselves and so sex becomes extraordinarily significant. It is used to gain God or one's personal pleasure and escape. The simplicity of perception is denied when we live according to a formula or an ideal.

'How am I to convey all this to a student?'

You will never ask that question if you have through self-observation seen life as a movement without broken pieces.

There is no 'how', no method. The sensitivity of intelligence will tell you what to do with the student.

'Mustn't we fulfil as men or women? A woman fulfils herself when she has a baby and cares for it. Sex is a fulfilment.'

I wonder what you are fulfilling: why you want to fulfil, and is there such a thing at all? Without putting these questions we just demand fulfilment like a child crying for the moon hoping it will be cheese. When you say you must fulfil, what is the urge behind it and who is fulfilling? The urge behind this is the desire to be, to become. What is it that seeks to be, to become, through some sort of fulfilment? Is it memory, the past, a bundle of words and ideas which is the ego, the 'me' that says I must fulfil? It is natural for a woman to have a baby, but when she says she can only flower in having a baby then she has built an image about herself as a woman, and that image demands fulfilment. The image is a formula or an idea, not the woman, not a sane, healthy, balanced woman. Or when you as a man fulfil yourself through your son or through some action, the 'you' is the image you have built about yourself, which is thought as knowledge. So you are living on words, on empty meaningless formulas. The what is *is far more important than your demand to fulfil. When you are free to see* what is *and not try to change it, find a substitute or escape from it, then you are free from* what is. *There is only the negation of fulfilment, and the beauty of it is in not being.*

The lean man sitting in the corner who had been listening very carefully, watching others and never committing himself, now shyly ventured out. 'Sir, surely you have omitted one thing, which is instinct, the bodily urge, the healthy functioning of the glands. It is this instinct that is in play, and given a free expression of that instinct there would be no problem. Remove all these taboos and inhibitions and it would be quite natural.'

Compulsive eating can also be called natural. One distrusts the word instinct. *There is the normal, natural, healthy human action but we distort it, poison it with the preoccupation of thought, by pictures, dress, pornography, the crude novels written by distorted minds, and so on. All these strengthen the neuroses of thought. It is strange that whenever human action is touched by thought with its formulas of pleasure and pain, with its images of what should be, all mischief is let loose. We don't see this. On the contrary, we worship thought. It is thought that has made the division of sex and no-sex, heaven and hell. Thought has created its own image which it worships, whether it is sex or the image of the saviour, the guru or the image of an ideology.*

The European who was wearing Indian clothes said, 'Do you mean to say that we must live without thought?'

Not at all, sir. Learning and understanding the structure and nature of thought is wisdom, and it is this wisdom of intelligence that acts.

40

WHAT DOES VIRTUE MEAN?

From the high mountains with their snow and glaciers, with their deep, dark-blue valleys with forests of pine, beech and elm, the little stream began. Passing many villages it became the great river feeding the parched land. Passing many towns, made dirty, polluted by human beings, it made its way to the sea. When the monsoon came with thundering rain the river would rise forty to sixty feet, sweeping everything before it, bringing fresh soil, a rich sediment in which the wheat was sown. You could see it across the river, fresh, green and sparkling.

The huge bull was there that evening, chewing its cud. It had a large hump and short, sharp horns. You stroked it and it didn't seem to mind. On the contrary, it seemed to like it. The bull would be chased out of the field by a boy. It went from field to field eating its way and each owner would chase it to the next field. So it kept going all day, fat, lazy, harmless. A few days later you would see it in another field as you went by. In the evening light it seemed threatening and wild but it was really quite tame, without violence. The next day it would be at the little temple with the cows.

Why do we make meditation so difficult, so complicated and formal? Why has it become something to be learned, a thing to be practised, pursued and sought? Why do we accept instructions about it from another, with method and reward? And is it meditation that you gain at the end of sacrifice, control and suppression? Is enlightenment a thing of thought, something put together, cultivated and nourished? A sannyasi sat on the riverbank with eyes closed, rigid, motionless, trying to control his thoughts, punishing himself in his damp robes which he had just washed. He was trying to capture something that had been told to him, something he had read in a book or been taught by his guru. Is this meditation? There are thousands upon thousands like him in this land, in solitude among the snow-capped mountains or sitting in a temple or a darkened room alone, battling with thoughts, shaping them by a series of other thoughts, a network of confusion. They will tell you that they are gaining insight, that they can control their thoughts completely, never realising the controller is part of the controlled. They are subtly proud of their achievement, or they have gained some kind of power to be exercised, to be the object of great wonder.

What has all this to do with meditation? You may be able to levitate, have the powers of extrasensory perception, tell people of their petty little future or heal them so that they can carry on with their empty lives. All this is not meditation. The effort, the practice, the gaining of visions, having some powers and collecting a lot of followers—this outward exhibition has nothing whatsoever to do with meditation. In all this there is danger, a hidden ugliness and the coil of secret conceit. Meditation is the most simple, natural thing, like the flow of water, continuous, persistent, whose depth is unknown. It is a living thing and cannot be put into the cage of thought with its schools of yoga, mantras and disciplines. If one would really meditate and know the beauty of it, one must set all this aside as one would put away all poison. This denial is not the action of will or decision but the simple observation of it. Just observe all this without any resistance. That very observation is the movement of meditation. You do not have to go to different countries or inquire from another to learn what it is.

Meditation is the understanding of the heart. When the heart cleanses the mind of all its tricks and absurd devices, its conceits and stratagems, meditation flows as clearly as the fresh waters of a river. Meditation is the movement of enlightenment, whether at the beginning or the end, for in meditation there is no beginning and no ending.

It was a cool morning. There was a nip in the air and the teachers in the room were warmly dressed. The man with the thoughtful eyes and clean-cut face said, 'Many students today are taking up psychology for they feel they can help people in this way. Often they wish also to study philosophy. The two seem to complement each other. Considering this, what place has religion in our studies?'

Another said sharply, 'Religion has no place in our modern life. One leaves all that to the old women.' He was almost angry that the subject should have been raised. 'What is more important is an ethical way of life, a humanitarian outlook.' He went on, 'How can one teach the moral principles? Without these principles life becomes chaos.'

Another asked, 'Why do you object to religion? The truly religious man is moral. Morality by itself has little meaning. It is like a pot; it's what you cook in it that matters, not what kind of vessel it is. Why be so antagonistic to the word? The intellectuals object to that word but one observes that as they get older and reach the brink of senility they become religious-minded and ardently espouse their belief. Our friend misses the point, I fear.'

Philosophy divorced from the religious way of life becomes merely theoretical, however cunning it may be. Institutionalised religion with its beliefs and dogmas is utterly meaningless and superficial, however splendid its ritual. The inquiry into the religious mind is far more important than the subtleties of philosophy. Man has always sought something that is not put together by thought; sought something that is imperishable; sought truth which is not opinion, which is not conjured up by one's conditioned demands and hopes. One observes the transiency of life and tries to find something that is not of time. This has been man's quest but unfortunately he gets caught in his own projections or those of others.

Surely you do not object to the understanding of a way of life in which there is no fragmentation as God and human, a total comprehension of existence in which morality is an undivided part. As our friend pointed out, morality by itself has no meaning. So can all of us here consider this question—not being for or against religion or this or that belief, but rather study and learn together about this question of virtue? Can we consider a way of life in which fear and its opposite, pleasure, are understood, and discover for ourselves if there is or is not a timeless dimension, which you may call by whatever name you wish?

Nodding his head vigorously in approval he said that this would be most worthwhile, both for ourselves and as teachers responsible for students. 'We are so disoriented—with a heavy tradition on one hand and on the other a permissive society with its affluence—that the mind gets utterly confused. One may logically support this or that, dialectically sustain one opinion or prejudice, but when one has seen all this in both action and theory, it seems to me one must ask these most fundamental questions. The traditional way of living we know so well in this country is going to pieces, and the system of the bureaucratic ways of life denies freedom and maintains conformity at all costs. Then there is the permissive society, letting go all values and traditions, doing what one likes whenever one pleases. One has observed all this; it doesn't demand great study and vast explanations. If we could apply our minds to the question which you have raised, sir, let us consider virtue and the understanding of a way of life in which a different dimension enters.'

Another who had not yet spoken said, 'I thoroughly agree with this, though unfortunately the word *religion*, not the thing behind it, has become something to be avoided. I personally would like to go into this question very deeply for I feel this is the source of all beauty and action. It has been said that we do not live by bread alone, and when bread becomes all important then all mischief is let loose.'

We sat quietly for a few minutes. There were many red flowers on the tree and one of them had fallen into the room. It had not faded, it was bright, clear, sharply designed. There was a faint scent of the jasmine. A bullock cart went by.

What does virtue mean? Is it a thing to be practised day after day, cultivating the moral excellence and uprightness of man, which gives him a certain power and authority? In the sense that we are using the word, is it the result of effort and determination, of resistance and compliance? Is virtue the result of overcoming that which is not virtuous, suppressing in order to conform, denying in order to achieve and attain? Is virtue born out of the conflict of duality? Or has virtue nothing to do with all this, neither with the conditioning of society, which is essentially immoral, nor dependent on environment, whether traditional or permissive? If one has a pattern of virtue and tries to carry it out in the friction, suppression and rivalry of daily life, it ceases to be moral excellence. A superficial order may be produced but inherent in the complicity of conformity is the disintegrating factor of disorder. The negation of what is considered moral—not as a reaction but through the observation of what actually is—*is the beauty of virtue, which is order. A blueprint laid out by a cunning mind or a gifted hand invariably denies order. Order is virtue. It is not according to any pattern, culture or system of society, but is the order that comes naturally and easily without the compulsion of conformity when one understands the whole field of disorder in which we live.*

'Are you saying, sir, that virtue can never be practised? You mean humility can never be practised, which is a fact. If you try to practise humility, vanity becomes more polished, more subtle and refined. Are you saying that through a disordered life with its contradictory disciplines one can never find moral excellence? And yet that is what we are trying to do. Through our confusion we are trying to be virtuous or moral and therefore it is, as you say, immoral. So are you suggesting that we come face to face with our disorder, understand it, study it, and out of this will flow the purity of excellence?'

As we said, virtue is a living thing, fresh every minute, not to be put in the prison of thought, tortured and distorted. Freedom—not from *anything but just freedom—is the essence of moral excellence. This freedom is in itself the beauty which we call virtue or order. This freedom implies great austerity; but it is not the austerity of the harsh practice of the saints or monks with their vows and suppressions. This virtue is not the outcome of discipline. It has no discipline. The virtuous man is a free man and therefore has no discipline, which is conformity. He lives in clarity without any confusion. The clarity of perception acts without will, which is resistance. Freedom is the clear perception of order which is essentially moral.*

41

ONLY THE UNDISTORTED MIND CAN SEE TRUTH

A strong wind was blowing from the west, bending the trees. The sea was restless; that morning the wind had brought huge waves breaking on the shore. The hills behind the house were green after the heavy rains. It is a part of the country where it doesn't rain very much but this year it had come in torrents. There were landslides and in front of the house, facing the sea, the earth was slipping. Everywhere there had been damage from the storms but the lakes would be full and there would be plenty of water for the coming summer. It is a beautiful land, full of promise, but there was pollution everywhere. Even the creatures of the sea were suffering, for everything flowed to the sea.

The mind is as restless as the sea. It is always occupied with something or other, with the kitchen or with God, with sex or the pursuit of pleasure. It is never quiet, and the fear of not being occupied becomes a problem.

The day before, at the next table, two old men had been talking. They were telling each other about their political life, about the people they knew, about their sons and about their daughters who had married well. They seemed to know the prominent government leaders under whom they had served and the owners of newspapers and their editors. They told anecdotes about these people for over an hour and you couldn't help overhearing what they were saying. During that hour they had not a moment without a word. People at the other tables were talking endlessly; they had to be occupied otherwise they would be shy or uncomfortable. Through talk they tried to establish a relationship that would cover up everything. It appears that the mind has to be occupied with something or other, is ever restless, always seeking some kind of expression. There is a fear of being alone, dissociated from everything. When you do walk alone you carry the burden with you, your problems, your enjoyments, the things you have done and the things you will do. This endless chattering seems to satisfy the mind. An occupied mind is a petty little mind, going round and round within the walls of its own thoughts. This isolation is not aloneness. To be alone implies freedom, freedom from the known. Then only can something new happen.

There were many teachers there that morning from many parts of the world. One of them who had already asked a question and had been pushed aside, again asked, 'If I may use the word *religion*, what place has it in the school and in our lives? And how can it be taught apart from the moral issue?'

Can the understanding of truth, which is religion, be divorced from moral excellence?

Another who had come a long way by ship, train and bus said, 'Is not the moral truth the only reality? We want to discuss religion without understanding morality and everyday living. As you have often said, conduct is the foundation upon which we can build, yet we spin on about God, theology and other things, without really bringing about in ourselves a way of living that is honest and true. We talk about God when we are really hypocrites and we want to teach others this hypocrisy. All theologians have a certain credo and around that they spin endless theories.'

He went on, 'It seems to me that as human beings and teachers it is our function to convey this moral excellence or virtue to those for whom we are responsible. How do we convey this? If we could start from there, perhaps we could enter into the field called religion. So I would like to ask all those who are here how to convey to the student his moral responsibility, integrity and an abiding honesty.'

The one in his usual corner replied, 'By our example, by our way of life, what we do, how we talk to our students.'

Isn't there a danger in becoming an example? You become a hero, you encourage imitation, conformity, and thereby destroy the other's integrity. History is full of examples: there are a thousand saints and the latest gurus. Though it denies hero worship the present generation has its own changing idols. In offering examples you deny them freedom. Surely it is far more important that they should understand their own patterns of behaviour, their own contradictions and confusions, rather than offering a particular pattern. The teacher and the student are both learning, learning about themselves, their conduct and the way they live. It is not that the teacher is totally honest and therefore can tell another what honesty is. It is rather that he can convey to the student that they are both learning what moral excellence is.

The man from overseas said, 'This becomes impossible when there is a division between us and the student. We feel we know better than they do. We sit a little higher and this superiority is a great satisfaction. You are denying us this if all of us are learning. It is very difficult for most of us to come off our perch.'

As we have said, there must be a firm foundation before we can build a house. The understanding of virtue, which is order and moral excellence, is at the same time building a house. Religion and morality are interrelated; they are not two separate things. Could we put the question this way: what is a religious mind that is learning the beauty of order? All religions are organised institutions based on propaganda. Each has a hero and his followers, its myths, superstitions, its idols or the bare walls of the mosque.

From childhood we are educated to believe, conditioned by the culture we live in, and this divides mankind. All this has nothing whatsoever to do with the religious mind, for if one really wants to find out what truth is one must be free from every form of belief, imagination and authority. Belief in the sacred is the outcome of fear, though one may call it the love of truth. Fear of insecurity and the desire for salvation or enlightenment is the basis of all this. The brain needs to be secure otherwise it cannot function sanely and healthily. As it lives in chaos and confusion, it seeks security in a belief, whether it is belief in the perfect state or the perfect God. It projects its own desire on the image it has created by its insistent demands for security. Can all this be brushed aside and the mind become free of its own designs of permanency, of a heaven which is not on earth?

Another said, 'Aren't you asking an impossible thing of us? Of course we are conditioned, as a Hindu by my culture or as a communist or Christian by those cultures. The gods of our culture are much more permanent than the impermanency of truth. We are afraid to let go of what we know.'

If you really understand the structure fear has created and its dangers, obviously you will let it go. We really don't see for ourselves the danger of division which institutionalised religions have brought about. When you hold to your gods and another to his saviour, though each one says to love your neighbour, this inevitable division breeds antagonism, wars, suspicion and fear. If you really see this, not intellectually but factually, with your heart, your mind, with your whole being, then the very perception of this danger is the action of freedom. But in the modern world none of this plays a very great part, neither religion, nor science nor the promised utopias. We want to enjoy ourselves, living from day to day, not worrying about the future or that immense thing called death. We are tired and we want to live a superficial, comfortable life. Seriousness, with all its significance, becomes a bore. But yet one has to be tremendously serious to throw off all the things that man has imposed upon himself through fear and the entanglements of pleasure. Without understanding these two there is no morality. Nor is there the bliss that is beyond enjoyment.

Again the man in his corner said, 'We are not deeply serious. Life has been "too much with us". We convey the dreariness of our own lives to our students or we are merely concerned with information and knowledge. The student is already worn out when he leaves the university. Those who drop out seem to have more energy but they waste it in useless activities, pleasurable or violent. You are really asking us, aren't you, to become innocent and see life as if for the first time, simply, clearly and with great passion? I lost all my passion long ago. Not that I am an old man but all this struggle, economically as well as inwardly, has drained me of my energy.'

Doesn't innocency mean a mind that is incapable of being hurt? Whatever happens around it, or the things it has been through, can never touch it, can never harm it. This is innocence. When it has not been injured, the brain, the mind, the heart, which are all one, has abundance of energy; the more you ask of it the more there is. It is only the undistorted mind that can see truth.

'But being wounded and distorted, what is one to do? The student too has been distorted. Both teacher and student have been hurt and they know only resistance. How are we to break this down? Our tragedy isn't in our not seeing the new but is in what we are. I don't want my son to be like me but I know it is inevitable. There may be minor changes but the structure will be the same. How can we transform ourselves and the students too?'

There is no 'how' but only the actual seeing of what is *and going beyond it. Love is the perception of* what is. *Not the sorrow of* what is—*sorrow is mischievous and dangerous and it breeds self-pity and hatred. Love is its own light and you need no other.*

PART THREE

EXPLORATIONS INTO MEDITATION

42

WHAT REALLY IS SACRED?

It was really a most beautiful morning. There was a slight mist over the trees and on the river. The sun wasn't up yet but would be in a few minutes. There were many fishermen in their little boats, in which they slept under a covering, dark shapes against the light of the water. It was still quiet; the noise of the city and the roar of the train across the bridge had not begun. Now the sun was coming up. You could see it just behind the trees, a great ball of golden red. In a minute or two it would be over the trees. It was now making a golden path on the water. As it was a very still morning without a breath, the mist lay on the river a little longer. The warmth of the sun would soon dispel it. Then you saw the river, wide, deep, a marvellous thing, full of ecstatic beauty, as still and wide as a lake.

Now the fishermen were going home to their nearby village with the night's catch. The gold on the river had gone; now it became molten silver, dancing, shimmering with the full light of the sun. You could not look at the sun itself, it was too strong, but you could look at the river with its brilliant light. And the beauty of that light would last all day, though the sun set behind the minaret in the noisy, dirty city.

The river was considered very sacred; more sacred than any other river. They literally worshipped it. They chanted about it in Sanskrit and in the many other languages that were part of the country. From the north to the south they knew and worshipped that river as ancient and holy. Many millions of pilgrims came throughout the ages to bathe in it and to have their sins washed away. They sat on its banks in meditation, in their wet clothes, until the sun warmed them; and they carried their meditation dreamily throughout the day. Many things were happening on the banks of the river, everything imaginable, and yet it was a sacred river, especially there where the river was very beautiful. The opposite bank was green with the winter wheat and the trees beyond. The little village with its white walls was hidden among the trees.

On the veranda two doves were cooing. They were beginning to build a nest in an alcove. Screeching parrots went by, flashing green, zigzagging along, never straight in their flight. A man across the river was calling to someone on this bank.

There were four in the room that overlooked the river. They looked very grave and serious. One of them said, 'I wonder if there is anything serious in life which is holy. I am rather sceptical about life being sacred, or the cow, or any object on the earth, including man.' Another said, 'The river is sacred because, first of all, it is beautiful, timeless, and it has been worshipped for thousands of years. I like beauty—the trees and the hills and the flowing waters—and that is sacred. Beauty is sacred, not only what man has put on the earth, as the temple, the cathedral and the marvellous things that have been made by the hand—the poems, the music, the sound of a flute. All these I consider most sacred, to be held dear and cherished.' The third one said, 'I know there is sacredness in the religious books which I read, in the revelations by the great masters, in the symbols, in the image personified in the temple, in the church or in the empty mosque. The idea, the supreme ideal, the image that you have in your heart of the supreme, which may be nameless, these I consider holy, most sacred, worthy of adoration. I often feel as I walk in the woods that I must be very careful not to destroy, not to break a leaf or pick a flower, not to hurt anything, not even to tread on a blade of grass. I feel this very strongly, for all this I hold most holy.'

A fourth who had been listening to the others said, 'Man is sacred, if one must use that word. Because he is sacred the gods he has invented are sacred. To kill a man is the most sacrilegious thing. The things he has made, however badly, however corrupt they are, behind all the mess and confusion that man has brought about in himself and outside of himself, in all his relationships, however brutal, callous, violent, there is a fine sense of the hidden sacredness. One cannot judge by outward appearance, words, gestures and acts only, because man has endured for thousands upon thousands of years. However disastrous his life he is timeless and so he is sacred.'

A train was crossing the bridge with the roar of steel upon steel. In the bright light of the sun outside the window you could see the strong current of the river.

Each person thinks or feels that one thing is sacred, the thing he holds most dear, whether it be an image, a symbol or a person. We all want in our unholy life something that is really worthwhile, profound, sacred. So we invest this feeling in the image that is in the church, in the temple or in the idea that the mosque holds. There is a deep longing to have something imperishable in our hearts that can never be destroyed by time. This we call holy or sacred. Ask each man and he will tell you that there is either nothing sacred in life, or he will tell you his own particular hope, fancy, longing, personified in an image, ideal or in the fantasy of a utopia. The books, the sayings of a saint, teacher or saviour become holy, to be worshipped, to be repeated with deep emotion, with ecstatic devotion.

When you observe all this without the eye of rejection, don't you ask what really is sacred? Is there such thing? What is sacred and what is action that is sacred? Action being living. To find this out, not verbally but with your heart, with your mind, with your whole being, because you understand the significance of it, you must put aside the word, the image, the symbol, the theory, the knowledge that you have considered sacred. You must put aside all these completely and utterly.

'Can I, a human being with my hopes, despairs and longings for something ecstatic or sacred, do this?'

You can make a stone into a holy or sacred thing. Thought can make anything sacred and holy but it is not necessarily then holy. Is thought in itself sacred, however subtle, however refined, however beautiful or noble it may be? Or is it merely a mechanical thing, a response to various forms of memories, experiences and knowledge, and therefore quite mechanistic and of matter?

You can or may call something holy or sacred. The human mind, with its tremendous longing for something that is imperishably beautiful, may call thought itself holy. But is it? To really find out or come upon it with your heart, one must discard everything that thought has created as sacred, everything that it has put together in the form of a book or everything that it has made by the mind or by the hand. All that must be set aside because man deceives himself so endlessly. The very illusion becomes sacred because he loves the illusion. The ugly can be made most beautiful by thought. The very evil, if one can use that word, can be made the most marvellous thing. So if the mind and the heart are to find what is the most sacred thing and the most sacred way of living, one must set aside all this utterly and completely.

'Then what is there?'

Then there is nothingness, complete emptiness. Not the emptiness that thought can fill. Not the emptiness and nothingness which thought can circumvent and build something out of. It is an emptiness which thought can never touch, for it is not the product of thought. It is not a mechanical thing—by doing this you will get that—it is not a marketable thing. It is this nothingness, total emptiness, that is. *And you may call it sacred, beautiful, true, divine, but the description is not the described. That is the only thing that can be lived.*

43

CHOICELESS AWARENESS AND ATTENTION

After many days of cloud and rain, mist and fog, the sun came out early this morning, bright and clear in a cloudless sky. After so many days of darkness the grass looked sparklingly green. Every leaf was laden with dew and the air was perfumed. There was a hint of autumn. On the bright green lawn there were long shadows and five wagtails bobbing up and down. In the distance two male pheasants were strutting, bright in the sunlight, their colours clear, their long tails gently sweeping the lawn. And beyond were the wooded hills with green slopes.

As you looked out, the mind was only observing, not recording, not even recognising the various trees and the many varieties of green, the sheep in the distance. It was extraordinarily still; there wasn't even a ripple of thought and the depth of that stillness was not measurable. It is measurable only when thought takes part. It is curious why the mind suddenly becomes, without any volition, absolutely still, empty of every thought, of every feeling, and yet in a state of observation. Meditation is the wrong word. Meditation implies a meditator, an awareness that he is meditating, experiencing, recognising, storing up. All this is a matter of measurement but now, watching the beauty of the land, the flying crows and that quiet dog on the lawn, there was no measurement as time and space, height or depth. Nothing else has no measurement.

What is the relationship between choiceless awareness and attention? What is attention? Does it come about through the act of will, through long practice, through any form of coercion, or does it come about naturally, without any effort?

To observe with choice is one thing and to observe without choice is another. The one leads to conflict and strife, the other to the clarity of understanding. To look without any reaction at the grime of the road and the tree that is beside it, just to observe them both without any differentiation and yet be aware of the bright grass and the dirty gravel. The constant choice, the discrimination between this and that—that which is ugly and that which is beautiful, reacting to both according to our sensitivity—is to be caught in the mere shallow movement of existence. To observe and to listen without any comparison or measurement gives to the mind a quality of vulnerability which is incapable of being hurt, and so incapable of hurting.

When you look out of the window and see the long shadows there is an attention which is both outer and inner. When there is this attention, the body naturally becomes extraordinarily quiet and all the activities of the brain, the recording and the reacting are in abeyance. Though it has accumulated a great deal of knowledge the brain itself seems to become free from it and can use it without the interference of the centre, the observer with all its egotistic activities.

In this attention space has quite a different meaning. The space of a room and the shape of the tree in space are both measurable. But the space of attention, having no centre and therefore no border, is not measurable. You cannot measure that which is totally empty. It is this emptiness that is aware, that is attention. It is this attention that can act without the impediment of the past.

Choiceless awareness is a movement in attention. They are not two separate things but they become separate when you are attempting to be aware or trying to pay attention. When there is a choice of action, the uncertainty of what to do, there is a division between awareness and attention. Choice exists only when there is uncertainty and therefore confusion. Action of clarity has no choice.

Is there attention during the sleeping hours? One can understand what this attention is during the waking hours: that peculiar watchfulness in which there is no centre from which you attend. In sleep the recording process is lessened when external objects do not impinge on the mind and the eyes are closed. But there is the activity of dreams, which is a continuation of our waking activity of problems, annoyances, violence and the demands for pleasure with its fears. Unless these are totally resolved dreams will continue. Attention then becomes rather superficial and meaningless.

During waking hours this cloud of sorrow and the confusion that man has collected over the centuries must be resolved before there is understanding of what attention is during sleep.

Attention gives to the mind a quality of youthfulness. In this attention time as age disappears altogether. In attention there can be no conflict whatsoever. It is strife, struggle and conflict, with their bitterness, anxiety and fear, that give age to the mind. Begin with the understanding of these things, and the freedom that brings. Total freedom from these is attention.

44

WHY DO YOU MEDITATE?

The hills were peaceful now; quiet, serene with that strange quality of aloofness. For the last five days a howling wind from the north was pushing at them and they seemed to be going before the wind. They have been battered. They have had fires when everything was burnt on them. There wasn't a single tree, bush or creeping vine that had not been burned black, grey and lifeless. They were stripped bare. All the animals had fled from them—the coyote, the rabbit, the deer and the bear.

Now they were back again after the rains. The hills were a lovely green but it would take years for any bush or tree to flourish. But in the clear morning air the lupin, the mustard, the ice plant and every green thing was unfolding to the sun. You felt very close to them, as close as two petals of a flower. You hardly dared to look at them for they were still shy, open, naked. As you passed by you were their friend; you too stood alone, distant and far away. In that aloof aloneness division came to an end.

It was a lovely morning, with the quail pecking on the lawn. They are shy birds and at the least movement they scuttled off into the bushes from which they would come hesitantly, slowly and scratch for the grain spread for them. There were about forty of them with their crests, fat little bodies and quick movement, the delicate shy movement of life. The city was far away across the blue Pacific bay. Somehow the hills and the sea were motionless and utterly silent. In that silence life began.

'Sir, I have gathered various systems of meditation from books and teachers. At first I picked haphazardly what pleased me or at least what I thought meditation should be—the Zen, the Hindu systems of meditation, the extremely subtle and the obvious and crude forms of sexual union, the repetition of mantras, the forceful silencing of the mind, the practices of ten minutes every day and increasing it week by week. I have not only played with them but made it a serious affair. I can see that through certain forms of concentration one can develop powers like clairvoyance and so on, but as you say these powers are like candlelight in the sun; they may be useful in darkness but they are totally irrelevant. I have always been attracted to meditation for I feel there is something in it that is strangely beautiful, and there are states of consciousness which calculated thought can never penetrate.

'The other day I heard a man on the radio talking about meditation, telling his audience what to do. I was really quite horrified by it; it sounded cheap and vulgar. I suppose you wouldn't consider me serious enough to go beyond the wall of vanity and ambitious achievement but I think I am serious. On this beautiful morning I don't want to disturb its beauty by endless chatter of silly questions. I don't want to tell others what meditation is or turn it into a profit. But I really would like to penetrate into this dimension to which meditation must open the door.'

Meditation is the ending of all decision, determination and choice, which are the expression of will. Will is the continuation of knowledge, of time, a movement from the known to the known. The action of will is resistance in concentration. To focus one's attention on an object of one's choosing is still the action of will as discipline, forcing the structure of thought by thought in a particular given direction. All this and more is the action of the will which is the observer. In meditation the observer has no place at all, so the understanding of the meditator is more important than meditation.

Why do you meditate at all? Is it to have a great experience, to reach another dimension, being bored with this one? Is it to overcome the destructive inertia of self-concern? Is it to lead a better life and is the better beyond the good? When you look at that yellow flower with beauty in your eyes is there not meditation? When your ear catches the note of a bird is that not meditation? Or the cry of a child, or the violence of a man with a bomb, is that not also the movement of meditation? When you watch you may see. If there is no love in your heart, how can there be meditation? Without the ending of sorrow, violence and conflict, how can the mind be utterly still?

Really it is not meditation that is the problem, it is the observer, the thinker who is everlastingly lifting every stone to see what is underneath. What he finds is what he already knows. The monotony of the experience of the thinker is the monotony of the known; the activity of the brain is within the field of the known. To see the truth of this is intelligence, and that intelligence then uses the known and is free of the known. This intelligence is not yours or mine; it has no heritage.

'I don't want to ask any questions, sir, but may I sit quietly with you for a few minutes?'

THE RELIGIOUS MIND IS THE
MEDITATIVE MIND

'I am an old man now but I have been concerned with a religious life from my youth. My wife died many years ago, my children are married, happily and unhappily, and there are many grandchildren. I have studied philosophies, joined religious groups, followed the living and the dead saints, been to the temple, to the mosque and to the church. Each man invents his own god or has a principle according to which he lives, or he plays with philosophical ideas. Somehow all these things have not revealed to me what a religious life is. The authorities have said it is this or that, prescribed certain ways of living, imposed beliefs. I have practised rituals, endless chants and hymns but the whole so-called religious structure has little meaning. It would be a marvellous thing at the end of my days to find out what is really a truly religious life! Is it of the mind? Doing good to others, being compassionate, seeing that one leads a fairly decent and moral life—does all this constitute a religious life?

'Of course you must know what the Vedantists say, which again seems to me an assumption, clever theorising and empty speculation. In all this, ideas and belief play an important part, perhaps the greatest part: that you must believe to be religious, that you must have an ideological purpose with its book of instructions: thou shalt, thou shalt not. I doubt if the saints were ever religious at all, or they merely followed tradition and the organised religions gave them sanctity as a reward for maintaining the tradition. Orthodoxy and respectability have played a great part in the so-called religious life. So, at the end of my life I am still asking what is truly a religious life.'

Would you say that religion is a way of life, which in its very activity reveals that which is sacred? That which is holy is not a thing of the mind, nor a calculated righteous activity. Surely it is not a life of vows and harsh abstinence. The brutal austerity of the monk or sannyasi cannot possibly lead to that which is sacred. One needs a mind that is free and sensitive, full of incalculable joy, to come upon the ecstasy which is not pleasure. So we had better start right from the beginning, denying and putting aside everything that man has invented in the hope of discovering that which is not measurable. Negation is the greatest act of reality.

'Can one negate everything? Is that possible? To negate everything is to negate myself, my whole conceptual existence, everything that has nourished my mind and activated my behaviour, my mode of conduct. If I deny all this what is left of me? Then I have no reason for existence at all.'

The 'me' is a word, a concept, a bundle of memories, the entity that believes, that seeks, that tries to live righteously, that has hope, fear, despair, that has endlessly measured itself against something nobler, greater, wiser. When this ego asks what a religious life is, can it ever know it or come upon something that is timeless, not of itself? It can know what is sacred only in terms of what it considers to be sacred, which is based on the past. Must not one negate all this to see that which is sacred? Would it not be better to lay the foundation for the freedom of such negation? Conduct obviously matters a great deal in itself—not as a means to an end, not to be good because it will bring a reward, but for the beauty of goodness itself. Can this be done? It means to be compassionate, without any motive, without any touch of social morality, which is self-conscious and therefore not compassion at all but pride. It means to be without fear at the deepest psychological level so that the mind is not caught in any illusion; to understand desire so that there is no contradiction in it; to bring about that delicate harmony in which the strife of the opposites has ended. It means to free the mind from psychological conditioning—which doesn't mean the ending of the natural conditioning of the brain—to lead a life of austerity in which every form of suppression, control and conformity is absent; to live with the discipline of intelligence without pursuing a pattern of habit. All this means the ending of the conflict. Then there is beauty and love.

The saints have denied beauty in every form for they think of beauty in terms of pleasure, and pleasure to them is sinful. The artist in expressing beauty has indulged in his vanity and pride. He exploits beauty. The money-maker is not interested in the consideration of what a religious life is. The man who is occupied with labour may occasionally think of it but only casually and indifferently. When all this is clear, not verbally or intellectually, can the mind then come upon that which is sacred? The religious mind is concerned with that which is sacred—to come upon it, understand it, live with it, to move with it, to go wherever it leads.

Of course, such a mind must gather the full meaning of what meditation is. Not that meditation is something different from all we have been saying. It is not different from compassion or the ending of fear, not different from austerity, freedom and the understanding of conditioning. Rather, it is going very deeply into all these things. All that we are doing now is truly meditation. At the beginning of this discussion you said all that is supposed to be religious is futile. You must also have discovered the futility of the mantras, trances and incantations, and all the other claptrap which the gurus and priests peddle. All that of course has no more to do with meditation than football and the circus.

So we come now upon something that is essential. A mind that has seen the truth of all this, and which is therefore in a state of meditation, has no centre from which it observes. It observes without conclusions and opinions. It is no longer in the conflict of becoming or not becoming. The religious mind is the meditative mind. It is only such a mind that is silent and that can come upon that which is sacred. The religious man is he who knows how to *live in this world with that silence. Religion is not the idolatry of the mind or of the image made by the hand. Living itself then becomes the most sacred thing. Living then is not separate from the state of mind that is silent.*

'I have listened very carefully and so I am learning. To repeat all you say will be meaningless to me and to others, and to interpret it becomes propaganda and is valueless. But I see after this voyage a glimmer of light which I hope is not the light of someone else or the word of someone else.'

46

OPINION IS NOT TRUTH

Meditation is the summation of all energy. It is not to be gathered little by little, denying this and denying that, capturing this and holding on to that. Rather, it is the total denial without any choice of all wasteful energy. Choice is the outcome of confusion; the essence of wasted energy is confusion and conflict. To see clearly *what is* at any time needs the attention of all energy and in this there is no contradiction or duality. This total energy does not come about through abstinence, through vows of chastity and poverty, for all determination and action of will is a waste of energy because thought is involved. Thought is wasted energy; perception never is. Seeing is not a determined effort and in this there is no 'I will see' but only seeing. Observation puts aside the observer and in this there is no waste of energy. But the thinker, who attempts to observe, spoils energy. Love is not wasted energy but when thought makes it into pleasure then pain dissipates energy. The summation of energy, of meditation, is ever expanding and action in daily life becomes part of it.

The poplar tree was being stirred by the morning breeze that came from the west. Every leaf was telling something to the breeze. Every leaf was dancing, restless in its joy of the spring morning. It was very early and the sun was not yet up. The blackbird on the lane was singing. It was there every morning and evening, sometimes sitting quietly looking all round and at other times calling and waiting for the reply. It would be there for several minutes and then fly off. Its yellow beak was bright in the early light. As it flew away the clouds were coming over the roof. The horizon was filled with them, one on top of the other as though someone had very carefully arranged them in neat order. They were moving and it seemed as if the whole earth was being carried by them—the chimneys, the television antennae and a very tall building across the way. The clouds presently passed and there was the blue spring sky, clear, with the light freshness that only spring can bring. It was extraordinarily blue. At that time of the morning the street outside was quiet. You could hear the noise of heels on pavement and in the distance a lorry went by. The sun would be up pretty soon and the day would begin. As you looked out of the window at the poplar you saw the universe, the beauty of it.

He asked, 'What is intelligence? You talk a great deal about it and I would like to know your opinion of it.'

Opinion and the exploration of opinion is not truth. You can discuss and carry on indefinitely with varieties of opinion, the rightness and the wrongness of them. However good and responsible, opinion is not the truth. Opinion is always biased, coloured by the culture, the education, the knowledge that one has. Why should the mind be burdened with opinions at all, with what you think about this or that person, or book and so on? Why shouldn't the mind be empty? Only when it is empty can it see clearly.

'But we are full of opinions. My opinion of the present political leader has been formed by what he has done. Without that opinion I would not be able to vote for him. Opinions are necessary for action, aren't they?'

Opinions can be cultivated, sharpened and hardened, and most actions are based on the principle of like and dislike. The hardening of experience and knowledge expresses itself in action, but such action divides and separates man from man. It is opinion and belief that prevent the observation of what actually is. The seeing of what is *is part of that intelligence you are asking about. There is no intelligence if there is no sensitivity of the body and of the mind, the sensitivity of feeling and the clarity of observation. Emotionalism and sentimentality prevent the sensitivity of feeling. Being sensitive in one area and dull in another leads to contradiction and conflict which deny intelligence. The integration of many parts into a whole does not bring about intelligence. Intelligence has nothing to do with knowledge or information. Knowledge is always the past; it can be called upon to act in the present, and it limits the present. Intelligence is always in the present and of no time.*

47

MEDITATION IS INTELLIGENCE

'Thought and emotion, all conflict, is so vast, so complex that you can never uncover it all. It is infinite in variety. Some of it goes back to our early childhood, lies hidden for forty years, suddenly to appear, summoned up from nowhere by a challenge. It is hidden, it is vast, it belongs to past and present, inextricably bound up together like the roots of some monstrous tree. How can we possibly deal with it? We can never uncover root by root. If we do act upon a single root it seems to thrive; resistance and interference give vitality to a problem. So I can never discover it all and can't even act upon that which I do discover because such action feeds it. How am I to deal with it?'

Doesn't it have a main root, the ego which feeds all the roots?

'How am I to bring out that main root, that central root? How am I to find it, discover it, deal with it? Besides, isn't it wrong to say that there is an ego and it acts through its roots? Each root is the ego, is bound to other roots; each detail contains the totality.'

Of course, the ego is not different from its root. Is there an action which will dry it up, which will not feed it, so that it withers and dies?

'It feeds itself, you don't have to feed it. It is self-feeding, self-perpetuating. Any action you do upon it irritates it, and inaction simply means that it continues to feed itself.'

Do we see that any positive action upon it feeds it and that negative action, non-action, also feeds it? Do we see this fully? Any action upon one root is an action of another root. All the roots are one root with a thousand shoots. Action and inaction are alike, equally futile. But if this thing simply goes on and on, feeding itself, growing, perpetuating itself, and if neither inaction nor action can stem it, does that mean that we are eternally condemned to live the self-perpetuating nightmare of these roots; conflict upon conflict, bred from our earliest childhood, with never a way out? This is hell! Is there any other action which does not belong to action or inaction?

'If one knew of such an action there would be no problem. So the answer is, I don't know.'

Don't be so hasty, so positive and aggressive about it. Even to ask the question whether there is another action that is not interference or inaction is the action of the root. If I see that, is there any problem at all?

'Of course there is a problem, the problem we started with. There are all these roots, all these actions of the ego and they are conflict. Action upon them is irritation and more conflict; inaction is simply allowing them to continue.'

We have been through a conflict and understood it.

'I haven't. The roots *are* conflict. One cannot brush the whole problem aside and do a disappearing trick on it by asking if there is any problem left at all. The problem arises each time my wife or my boss insults me. When I walk through that door nothing is changed and the slightest challenge makes the whole structure of the roots surge up again.'

We are not trying to do a trick, to verbalise the problem into non-existence. To continue, do I see the enormousness of the roots? Do I see that they are infinite, that they are joined together, that they stem from the beginning of time, that they are hidden?

'Yes, I see that they are like that. I see the fact of their infinity. But I do not see the actual roots themselves.'

That's right. Do you see the fact that they are so? Do you see the fact of them, their structure, their anatomy, their autonomy, their self-perpetuating, self-feeding action? Do you feel this fact really and truly with your very marrow? Can you touch it?

'Yes.'

And do you see in the same way that any action is another root acting to perpetuate the whole structure of the plant? And do you see that inaction is the same?

'Yes.'

Even to ask if there is any other action is the feeding of the roots. Whatever you do to interfere, to suppress, cut off, search or question with regard to these roots, it is the same as the action of the roots themselves—jealousy, greed, anger, fear and so on.

'Yes, I see all this clearly. This seeing is the action of understanding, and when understanding operates the root does not operate.'

Yes, that's it! That is all. Don't say another word. Instead of understanding *say intelligence. When intelligence operates then the roots do not operate. That is the end of it.*

'But the root sometimes has more vitality than intelligence does.'

There is no conflict between intelligence and the roots. All conflict is among the roots themselves, so there is either intelligence or the action of the roots, which is conflict.

'Now, where does love come into all this?'

This intelligence is love. This intelligence is meditation. Meditation is intelligence, which is still in action, which is love.

48

MEDITATION IS THE ESSENCE OF ENERGY

There was sunshine on the grass and the breeze was among the leaves. It was really a very pleasant morning, full of light, great beauty and quietness, a sense of deep, abiding peace. It was in every tree, in every bird, on the water and among the villagers who walked in deep shadows along the avenue under tall beeches.

He was a lean man, full of vitality and with a deep enquiring mind. He said he had been studying meditation for many years, trying to practise it according to various schools of thought and meditation but somehow he felt they didn't quite satisfy him. He felt that they missed something. So he was there that morning.

'I think we can leave most of the superficial meanings of meditation,' he said, 'but I would like this morning very much to go into the deeper meaning or deeper sense or feeling of meditation. I have practised many forms of meditation including the Zen system. There are various schools teaching awareness and attention but that becomes routine, monotonous and rather deadly. So we can leave all that aside.'

We must also set aside the whole meaning of authority because in meditation any form of authority, whether one's own or that of another, becomes an impediment and prevents freedom, freshness, newness. So authority, conformity and imitation must be set aside completely, otherwise you merely follow what has been said and imitate, which makes the mind dull, stupid. In this there is no freedom. So it is essential right from the beginning to put aside completely all authority, even your own past experience which may guide or direct. Then only can we really go into this very deep and extraordinarily important thing called meditation.

'I think I can follow that too. I have tried during these many years to see that I do not become a slave to somebody else's authority or to a pattern. I think I'm pretty sure of that but of course there is a danger that I may be deceiving myself. As we go along probably I shall find out. So I would like to ask, when you say that meditation is the very essence of energy, what do you mean by the words *energy* and *meditation*?'

Every movement of thought, every action demands energy. Whatever you do or think needs energy. That energy can be dissipated through conflict, through various forms of unnecessary thought, emotional pursuits and sentimental activities. Energy is wasted in conflict; the conflict that arises in duality—the 'me' and the 'not me', the division between the observer and the observed, the thinker and the thought. When that wastage is no longer taking place there is a quality of energy that can be called awareness, an awareness in which there is no judgement, evaluation, condemnation or comparison, but merely an attentive observation, seeing things exactly as they are both outwardly and inwardly without the interference of thought which is the past.

'This I find very difficult to understand. I find it extremely difficult to see things without the interference of thought. If there was no thought at all, would it be possible to recognise a tree or my friend, my wife or my neighbour? Recognition is necessary, is it not, when you look at a tree or the woman next door?'

When you observe a tree or the woman next door, is recognition necessary? When you look at a tree, do you say it is a tree? You just look. If you begin to recognise it as an elm, an oak or a mango tree, then the past interferes with direct observation. In the same way, if you look at your wife with all the memories of annoyances, irritations, pleasures, insults and so on, you are really not looking at her at all but only at the image that you have in your mind about her. So that prevents a direct perception. Direct perception does not need recognition. Recognition may be necessary, of your wife, your house, your children, your neighbour, but when you look, why should there be the interference of the past in the eyes, the mind and the heart? Doesn't that prevent you from looking clearly? After all, when you condemn or have an opinion about something, that opinion or that prejudice prevents or distorts your observation.

'Yes, I see that. I see that subtle forms of recognition do distort. I quite understand that. And you say all those forms are a waste of energy. Perhaps that is so, but I'm not quite clear on this point until I actually do it. And here begins the difficulty: to observe without naming, without any form of recognition, condemnation, judgement; for the naming, recognition, condemnation, as you point out, are a waste of energy. All right, that can be seen logically, perhaps, and actually understood.

'Then the next point is the division, the separateness that exists, or rather, as you put it, the space that exists between the observer and the observed, which creates a duality. You say that is a wastage of energy because it brings about conflict. I find what you say is logical but I find it extraordinarily difficult to—I don't know how to put it—to remove that space, to bring about a harmony between the observer and the observed. How is this to be done?'

There is no 'how'. The 'how' means a system, a method, a practice, which becomes mechanical and which we already have said is a wastage of energy. So we will have to get rid of the meaning or the significance of that word how.

'I am sorry to use that word again, but how is it possible? Again that word *possible* implies a future, an effort, a striving to bring about harmony. But one must use certain words and I hope we can go beyond these words. So how is it possible to bring about a union between the two, the observer and the observed?'

The observer is always interfering, always casting its own shadow upon the thing it observes. So one must understand the nature and the structure of the observer. Not how to bring about a union between the observer and the observed but rather understand the movement of the observer. In that understanding, perhaps the observer comes to an end. So we must examine what the observer is. The observer is the past with all its memories, conscious or unconscious, its racial inheritance, its accumulated experiences which are called knowledge, its reactions. In essence the reality is that the observer is the conditioned entity, the one that asserts always that 'I am'. And in protecting itself, it resists, dominates, seeks comfort and so on. The observer then sets itself apart as something different from that which is observed, outwardly or inwardly. This brings about a duality and from this duality there is conflict, which we said is a wastage of energy.

To be aware of the observer, the movements of the observer—the self-centred activity, assertions, prejudices—to be aware of all these conscious and unconscious movements which build the separation, the feeling that the observer is different. To be aware without any form of evaluation, without like and dislike; just to observe it in daily life, in its relationships. When this observation is clear, is there not a freedom from the observer?

'You are saying that the observer is really the "me", the "I", the ego. You are saying as long as that "I" exists, he must divide, separate, for in this separation, in this division, he feels alive; it gives him vitality to resist, to fight. To that battle in life he has become accustomed and that is his way of living. You are saying that this "I" must dissolve through observation, in which there is no sense of like or dislike, opinion, judgement, evaluation; just to observe this "I" in action. But can such a thing really take place? Can I look at myself so completely, so truly, without any distortion? And you say that when I do look at myself so extraordinarily clearly, the "I" has no movement at all. And you say this is part of meditation, don't you?'

Of course, this is meditation.

'This observation surely demands extraordinary self-discipline.'

What do you mean by self-discipline? Do you mean disciplining the self, putting him in a straitjacket, or do you mean learning about the self—the self that is the 'me', the self that asserts, that is dominant, that is ambitious, violent and so on? The learning about it is in itself discipline. Learning is discipline, for that word discipline *means to learn. And when there is learning— not accumulating—when there is actually learning, which needs attention, that learning brings about its own responsibility, its own activity, its own dimension. So there is no imposition upon it as a discipline, as something imposed. Where there is learning there is no imitation, no conformity, no authority. So if this is what you mean by that word self-discipline, surely then there is a freedom to learn.*

'I can't quite come with you where this learning is concerned. I see very clearly now that the "me" as the observer must come to an end. It is logically so. I think it is necessary so that conflict doesn't exist. That is very clear. But you are saying that in learning there is accumulation and this accumulation becomes the past. Learning is an additive process, but you are apparently giving to it a different meaning altogether. From what I have understood, you are saying that this very observation is learning and that learning is a constant movement without accumulation. Is that so? Can there be a learning without accumulation?'

Learning is its own action. What we generally do is to act upon what we have learned, so there is a division between the past and the action, and hence there is a conflict between what should be *and* what is, *or between* what has been *and* what is. *We are saying: can there be action in the very movement of learning? That is, learning is* doing; *not having learned and then acting. This is very important to understand because having learned,* accumulated, is the very nature of the 'me', the 'I', the ego. The 'I' is the very essence of the past and the past is impinging upon the present, into the future. In this there is constant division. But where there is learning, which is a constant movement, there is no accumulation which becomes the 'I'.

'In the technological fields there must be accumulated knowledge, otherwise one can't go to the moon, drive a car or do any of the things that one does daily in the office or at home. There accumulated knowledge is necessary.'

Of course, that is absolutely necessary. But we are talking about the psychological field in which the 'I' operates. The 'I' can use technological knowledge in order to achieve a position, a prestige. The 'I' can use that knowledge to function, but if the 'I' interferes in function there is inaccuracy and things begin to go wrong, because the 'I', through technical means or through function, wants status, position. So the 'I' is not concerned with the accumulated knowledge in the scientific field but it is using it to achieve something else. It is like a musician who uses the piano in order to become famous. What he is concerned with is fame, not with the beauty of music in itself, for itself. We are not saying that we must get rid of technological knowledge. On the contrary, the more there is that kind of knowledge the better for living and so on; but the moment the 'I' uses it, things begin to go wrong.

'I think I am beginning to understand. You are giving quite a different meaning and dimension to the word *learning*, which is really quite marvellous. You are saying meditation is a movement of learning so that there is freedom to learn about everything, not only meditation but about the way one lives, one drives, one brushes one's teeth.'

The essence of energy is meditation. As long as there is a meditator there is no meditation. However, the meditator trying to understand himself is part of meditation. But when he is attempting to achieve a state described by others, or in rare moments of a flash of experience, such...

'If I may interrupt you, sir—are you saying that learning must be constant, must be a flow, a line without any break, so that learning, action and meditation are one, are a constant movement? I don't know what word to use but I am sure you understand. Are you saying that the moment there is a break between learning, action and meditation, that break is disharmony or conflict, and in that break there is the observer and the observed and hence the wastage of energy?'

Yes, this is what we mean. Meditation is not a state, it is a movement, as action is a movement. As we said, when we separate action from learning, the observer comes in between the learning and action. Then he becomes important, not learning and action; then he uses action and learning for ulterior motives. So when it is very clearly understood that it is one harmonious movement—the learning, the acting, the meditating—in this there is no wastage of energy. And this is really the beauty of meditation. There is only one movement.

Learning is far more important than meditation or action. To learn there must be freedom, complete freedom, not only consciously but deeply, inwardly, a total freedom. And in freedom there is the movement of learning, acting and meditation as a harmonious whole. The word whole *means not only healthy but holy. So learning is holy, acting is holy, meditation is holy. This is really a sacred thing and the beauty of it is in itself, not beyond it.*

49

LIFE IS AN EXTRAORDINARILY BEAUTIFUL MOVEMENT

'I hope you don't mind my coming back again. I thought a great deal about what you said with regard to energy and meditation. I think I am beginning to understand what you mean by learning, meditation and freedom, but I don't quite grasp the full significance of what you mean by energy. I have been to monasteries and followed systems of meditation practices in India. From what I have read and have practised, they all advocate, at least in principle, the cultivation or gathering of energy so that this energy is directed and made whole. That energy must not be wasted through sex and so they advocate celibacy very strongly. The sannyasis in India and the monks of Europe have maintained this standard of conduct. For them it is essential to be celibate. I thought I would come this morning to talk with you about this question of energy which we human beings seem to waste in so many ways.'

It was such a lovely morning. The sun was clear in the sky and though it was autumn the leaves were still green. The shadows were very long. There was peace among the leaves, on the faces of the people and on the water. The air was of late summer and the beauty of the earth, the soil and the water was on the land.

'The monks have advocated that to reach the highest, one must have a life of celibacy, a life in which all your energies are dedicated to the realisation of the supreme. To me, living in this world with a family and doing business, how can I lead a life of celibacy? Isn't sexual desire part of the human being, as any other desire or wish? How can I cut it off? It's

Life is an extraordinarily beautiful movement

like cutting off an arm or plucking out an eye. How can I live in this world and reach the supreme? It is obvious that energy is necessary for all this and so one asks how this energy is to be gathered together.'

Everything we do needs energy—to go to the office, to walk down the street, to talk, to look at the sunset or watch the light on the water. And if you say to yourself that sex is a waste of energy, as religions have maintained, then you must withdraw not only from the demands of sex but also from looking at the trees, the face of another, the curve of the hills and the folds of the mountains and valleys. You must deny all that to conserve what you call this energy that is demanded to reach the supreme.

'Are you saying that one need not control the appetites, the senses, the sexual urges? Where is one to draw the line between indulgence and control? Where is one to restrain and where is one to let go?'

The monks throughout the world may deny the outward expression of sex but inwardly they are tortured human beings, fighting their physical urges, struggling against pleasure, restraining themselves from looking at the beauty of the world. Have you ever noticed that when monks walk they don't look around? They don't see the mountains, the hills, the flowing rivers, or listen to the birds. They are occupied with words, with books, with concentration, because they are basically afraid. For them to see is to invite pleasure, and so they resist. This resistance is a part of the struggle and conflict; the very resistance is a wastage of energy.

'Are you saying that we must have no control whatsoever?'

Not at all. We are not talking about control or resistance. We are trying to understand the whole problem of sex, the problem of pleasure, pain, and the delight in watching something that is beyond words, in looking at the height and depth of the mountains. But we are conditioned to accept the tradition, the authoritarian point of view. What we are trying to point out is that every form of control, suppression, imitation or conformity is an absolute waste of energy for it breeds conflict between what is *and* what should be. *It brings about a duality, a contradiction. Contradiction and duality are the spending of energy uselessly, wastefully. If you understand, really see the truth, the basic reality that control, suppression, conformity in any form is wastage of energy—not intellectually or just accepting the idea of it but seeing the deep truth of it—then your whole way of looking at it is entirely different. You would not approach this question of sex with fear or with pleasure or indulgence.*

Life is a movement, a constant, continuous, extraordinarily beautiful movement. When we lose this movement we then learn to accept resistance, barriers, controls, and so we live a life of torment. Being tormented, living in a battlefield that we call life, then as sex is perhaps the only pleasure and freedom that we have, we say to ourselves that we must control, indulge or suppress, or escape from it into an isolated monastery or live by ourselves, withdrawn from the world. Surely all this is utter waste of energy, is it not?

'I can see that, but I can see it only as an idea, as something outside. I don't feel it inwardly. It is not a reality to me, something vibrating, close, intimate. So what am I to do to move away from the traditional into the non-traditional, into this world of life which is everlasting movement?'

I don't think you can do anything. All that you can do is to observe. To observe there must be freedom to observe and to listen; to listen to your sexual demands, to observe the restraints you place upon yourself or your indulging or letting everything go, your living a life of constant conflict, battle, misery, confusion. Just observe all that—your control, your fears. Watch your sexual delights, the pleasures, not only your sexual appetites but the pleasures of flattery, of ambition, of greed, of cruelty and violence. Watch the fears of restraint. Watch the beauty of the earth and of the solitary tree on a hill. Watch this all as a whole, not seeing sex and pleasure or the tree as something separate, as a fragment apart from the rest of life. Watch the whole movement, in the office, the family, the pleasures of position, prestige and power which bring the fears, frustration and the demands for fulfilment. Watch all of this as a whole movement, not in fragments but a total, living movement.

Then you will see that your approach to this whole problem of living, including sex, family, responsibility, technical work, the office, fears, love, death, beauty, ugliness and sorrow, has quite a different movement. But to watch so closely, to be in complete communication with what you are watching, there must be no observer, for the observer is the past, is the tradition, that creates the space, the time interval between itself as the observer and the thing observed. This division is the very essence of conflict. Watch all that, listen to all the subtle, secret movements of conscious and unconscious desires, pursuits and demands. Watch them all as a whole, and in this watching or out of this watching comes quite a different action, quite a different a way of looking at sex and all the rest of it. This watching has great beauty in it, for this watching is the very essence of love and care. But if you merely suppress, control, fight, make life into a battlefield, then every action in that field is a wastage of energy. You need great energy, tremendous energy to watch. After all, love is a summation of this energy, for love is freedom—not an idea of freedom but actual freedom. This freedom comes only when you have watched every movement of your being, when there is never a statement of 'I am' or the feeling of 'I am'.

Well now, you have heard all this for the last two days. Having heard, having listened and watched, if there is no action then deterioration begins. Seeing the truth of something and not acting upon it is the way of deterioration and degeneration. To see is to act without the interval between the seeing and the acting. In any danger there is instant action; there is no interval between perception and action, and in that there is sanity. Sanity is sensitivity. It is the highest form of intelligence. So, acting in the battlefield is one thing and the action of seeing or listening is quite another. One leads to great sorrow, the other to beauty, love and freedom.

'May I ask a question? The conflict, the battle of life also demands energy, is part of energy. The other thing, this movement as a whole, are these two different? The energy that is demanded, that is necessary to fight, and the energy in which there is no fight whatsoever but a movement—are these two different or are they the same?'

Energy is the same. One can waste it in conflict, in destruction, in setting fire to the house in which you are living, which is the world. When one understands that energy and the wasting of it, when one observes it, listens to the burning, sees the flames, the destruction, the ugliness of it all, and observes it closely, attentively, that is also energy. And out of this observation, out of this listening, there is the other movement of energy in which there is no conflict, no battle; there is never a burning. One is destruction and the other is a movement of creation. But both are energy. The wise man moves away from the one to the other. The wise man is one who is not aware of himself as separate, for in that separation there is destruction, there is war, there is conflict, there is sorrow. When there is the absence of the 'me', the 'I am', and the battle that goes with it, which is part of this energy, there is that movement of life which is everlasting.

As we said, watching is learning and learning is always whole. Learning is a movement that is endless.

50

WHAT IS IT TO BE AWARE?

It had been a long, cold, tiring winter and every tree and bush was waiting, longing for the sun and the spring. The birds were already here, building their nests, calling to each other, claiming their rights. A pheasant, full of colour and rather cocky, with its long tail and its head up, was there every morning. It seemed to own the bushes and the lawn. It was an extraordinary sight to see it walking across the lawn on that foggy morning. The bushes and trees were bursting with life, leaf by leaf, after the dreary winter.

In the room there were African violets, a blue hydrangea and a chrysanthemum. It was the largest room, peaceful, quiet, restful, far away from all the noise, a room in which there has been no disturbance. Occasionally you heard a plane going by but somehow that did not disturb. As you watched out of the window you were aware of the great beauty of the land, the copper beeches with tender leaves, the flowering cherry. The daffodils were just fading. The lawn was becoming greener, richer and purer, and the trees were covering themselves with new fresh leaves so delicate and vulnerable. It was really a most peaceful, beautiful land that nothing seemed to have disturbed for centuries upon centuries. All the wars that it had faced seemed never to have touched it.

As you watched silently you were aware, with the stimulus of the mind, of the rich ploughed fields and the woods beyond. The horizon seemed to be just there, so close, where the earth and the sky met. There was a light which the fog had not concealed. You were aware not only of the beauty of the land but also of the much greater things, the wide, limitless expansion that went beyond the earth and the heavens, that seemed to have no limitation, no frontier, no border. It was an awareness of an observation without a centre and therefore without limitation. With its capacity to extend and expand, it wasn't a consciousness with limitations as we know it. It was not the consciousness of remembrance, of memories, of all the accumulated knowledge with its strife and enmity, pleasures and pain. It was beyond all that. It was an awareness of a different dimension, whose quality had the quickness of water, the beauty and love of something that thought has never touched, the sacredness of movement and not the solidity of a rock. It was not a fancy nor imagination, for awareness had put away all fanciful desires, demands and longings. It was an awareness which knew measure and so was able to go beyond it, above it, to the immeasurable which was not the opposite of the measurable. Without measure the world wouldn't exist, and yet the immeasurable was not the measure of the word, of thought.

As you looked out of the window on that foggy morning there was an awareness of all this, the pheasant on the lawn, the new leaf, the fading daffodils, the enormous richness of the land, the crows calling, the fields, the trees, the immensity of the earth, and *that which is*. *What is* is not the end. *What is* indicates, if you are aware, what is beyond that. So in this awareness all this seemed to be contained. And yet the awareness was not its content. The quality of perception is not that it perceives; the quality has nothing to do with perception. Light is light, not the quality of light—like love.

So there it was, that foggy morning, which would soon give way to a bright day and there would be rejoicing.

'Though you must have been asked this many times, I would really like to understand what awareness is. I would be very glad if you would go into it step by step, remembering that some of us have never even inquired into it or asked what awareness is. Some may have practised a kind of awareness read about in books or taught in a monastery. Some may have heard you and want to capture it through your feeling for it. So I would be most happy if you would tell me very simply what it is to be aware.'

I do not know why we make it all so difficult, why we want to complicate things, why we feel we must learn about it from another, why we want to practise, achieve a certain state of attention. All this seems such a vain, absurd desire for success or achievement. To be aware of this urge, this desire for enlightenment, the desire to be totally aware, just to be aware of it, is enough. The very simplicity of it shows the nature of awareness.

But since we want to go into it step by step, let's do it. Be aware of how you are sitting in that chair. Don't correct it, don't change your posture, just be aware how you have you crossed your legs, how you are stooping forward, trying to catch the meaning of what is being said, preparing yourself to understand. Just watch that. When you so become aware you want to correct your posture, you want to sit straight. Or you may ask what is wrong with crossing one's legs or leaning forward. Or you may be indifferent, asking yourself if it really matters how you sit. You are rationalising your particular habit. Just simply be without any recrimination or justification. Just watch. Then watch that hydrangea, be aware of it without the word, without like and dislike, and be aware of that dislike or like. Be aware of the proportions of the room, of that old table, the pot of flowers and the red wastepaper basket. Be aware of all this outward environment. Be aware of the trees beyond the room, the fields and the birds, without any interference of thought—thought being the word, the judgement, the condemnation or justification.

You will say that it is very difficult to do this because you have been conditioned. You have always thought that way; you look with the eyes of condemnation or justification. So be aware not of the fields, the trees, the room, the flowers, but of your condemnation or justification. Move away from the outer to the inner. Be aware of your conditioning. Don't try to alter it, don't try to shape it, don't try to suppress it, to do something, just be simply, quietly, aware of your state of mind that looks.

'There seems to be a problem with the attention span. I look at any of the things you've mentioned and my mind moves from that to the consciousness of my own inner working, my own conditioning, showing itself; and each bit of this awareness leads to a further association. So I find I am going from steppingstone to steppingstone in my mind, from one association to another. This is an endless thing.'

Now, is it endless? You make a definite assertion that it is endless and therefore you make it endless. You have already made up your mind that it can never be ended.

'No, I do not accept this as something inevitable, I'm merely describing something that happens. I can see the possibility of endlessness in this and therefore my mind seems to pull back and consider the fact of conditioning, the fact of endless association, and I am then aware of a process in my mind.'

Yes. Awareness is not a process, is not mechanical. Process implies a mechanism, and this is not. When you say, 'I move from association to association,' aren't you saying that you have not been aware of the first association? Be aware of the first association, not of the process, not of the sequence. Be aware only of how the mind works in association, not of the next step.

'In other words, be aware of the first link in the chain and see the chain.'

That's all. If you are aware of the first link you see the whole chain. But what you are doing is being aware of the whole chain without the first link, following the chain one link after the other to make a long, endless chain.

'Are you saying that I must be aware of the chain without

allowing the first link to appear?'

No, on the contrary.

'It is the first link that makes me see the chain.'

Yes. So look at the first link only and not the rest of the chain. So when you look at the first link, that is what is. *And that* what is *is not static. But when you make it into an endless chain it is without a movement; then it becomes mechanical; then you say it cannot be changed and you become hopeless and you remain with the chain.*

'Sir, if I may say this here, what you are describing I think is where psychoanalysis goes off into an endless pattern. What you are saying is entirely different. This is something quite crucial, I think. So could we go back? We see that first link and that only, and that is *what is*.'

That is what is. *Be aware of that, be aware of the first association, of how your mind associates; and the next movement is to associate that with the next.*

'Yes. That is the movement of thought.'

That's right. Whereas if you are aware of the first movement, do not put an end to it, don't remain there. You will remain there if you condemn it, justify it, if you observe it as an observer different from the thing observed. And this is where our difficulty comes in. So, have we understood each other so far? Let's be quite sure of this because if you are not sure we can go back.

'May I question you just a little more to be sure I am following correctly? When you see that first link, are you saying that is *what is* and that is what ends the thought process which would have gone on indefinitely?'

Partly, yes.

'Yes. I want now to touch on the question of the observer and the thing observed. Is that awareness of the first link the ending, in that instant, of the separation between the observer and the thing observed? Does it end it, for that moment? In that movement there is no observer?'

Don't bother about ending it. You have to understand much more than merely the ending of it.

'You see clearly the first link which is the bud of the thought process. And seeing that you withdraw from that, as from...'

No. Let me explain again. First of all let's understand what is. What is is the first link. And that first link, if you don't condemn or justify it, just observe it, you will see that it is. *And the truth of it is the movement in it.*

'In it? What do you mean by movement in *it*?'

In what is. But what is becomes static and therefore without a movement when you look at it as an observer and the thing as the observed. As long as there is a division between the observing and the thing observed, as long as there is that division, what is becomes like a rock, without any movement. But when there is no observer then there is the movement from that very thing, from that very rock of what is. Now I'll show it to you. There is the first association of like or dislike, the first link of hate or anger.

'It doesn't have to be anything like that. It can be just red, blue.'

Yes, just an ordinary thing, red or blue. Can you look at that red without naming, without allowing associations to arise from that, and look at that red without the observer?

'Yes, but I think it must be different from what you are describing because I can look at something without the thought process starting and continuing its chain, but sooner or later it starts up, maybe with a fresh subject. I can look very quietly at something and just look at it and not think about it, not have a chain.'

Let's be simple about this. We are looking objectively at that flower and you can look at that flower without naming, without like or dislike. That's fairly simple. That observation may last a second or ten minutes. There is an observation of objective things without the interference of thought or knowledge.

'Sir, it seems to me there is a danger in this. In this

experience of just looking without any thought process, it is just a very low level.'

It is a very low level.

'I am not taking in any great whole of anything nor being particularly aware, I am just sitting quietly without any particular thought, staring at a flower.'

Obviously it has no value. It doesn't touch you emotionally or it doesn't hurt you so it is not very important. But you can look at it that way. The difficulty arises when you look at yourself.

'When I look at myself it is one fragment or a torrent of fragments in rapid succession.'

Yes, that is the difficulty. To look, to observe or to be aware of one fragment.

'But in this there seems to be a very large difficulty. There is the objective flower that the eye perceives. It has an image on the brain. But when I look at myself there is no objective thing. Therefore to look at myself, what does the mind perceive? It can perceive either something totally unknown which is the whole—and I haven't the remotest idea what the whole of me is—or I seize on a portion, a finger, a hand or leg, in the inner sense. In other words, I think of myself and the first association is the finger that I catch hold of. What else is there? It can only be an image or a fragment of an image of something I call 'myself.' What do I look at? What is there to look at?'

You look at the image you have about yourself.

'But that is a series of fragments, incomplete.'

I know that. Take one fragment of that image, not the whole image.

'I don't know what the whole image is.'

Therefore don't bother about it, just take one fragment. One fragment. Can you be aware of that fragment without any association, without condemning it or justifying it, just be aware as you are aware of that flower, without like and dislike? Just to be aware of it. In that awareness you begin to discover how you are looking at that fragment. Are you looking at it as an observer, from the outside, as though you had no relationship with it? Or are you looking at it without the observer and therefore it is no longer a fragment?

'As you speak, I am aware of a sense of pain, of trying to understand and follow you. I am within it. I am not looking and saying, "I am feeling pain." I am feeling pain, therefore I am inside a fragment.'

Why should you feel pain? You don't feel pain when you look at that flower.

'No, because the flower is out there.'

Yes. Therefore why can't you look at that fragment without pain? It is a fragment.

'Because the fragment that I picked up, as you spoke, was one of pain.'

Look at it. Why do you call it pain*?*

'Because it is organically painful.'

Why? Please go into it. Why is it organically painful?

'Because I am trying something difficult: to understand what you are saying.'

Don't try. Don't try to understand what one is saying but just observe what you call the fragment which is painful. Just observe it.

'But what is this quality of observation? If the fragment is pain, either one feels the pain or one is being utterly verbal and intellectual, saying, "Oh, pain." Which is thought.'

No, no. How do you look at that pain?

'You look at it with your mind and body and everything. Which is that you feel it.'

You feel it. Now how do you feel it? Do you feel it as something apart from yourself?

'No. I feel it is the very marrow of myself.'

Yes, you feel it entirely, without the division.

'The division between what and what?'

Between the pain which you want to get rid of—and therefore a division.

'I am not saying I want to get rid of it.'

No, do look at it please, just go slowly.

'I am trying to feel something. It is like feeling water. It doesn't mean you want to pull your hand out of the water; you feel it.'

No, no. Please listen. There is pain. You feel pain when you look at that fragment, which happens to be pain. Are you looking at it with association?

'No I am not, and I am not trying to withdraw from it.'

You are not escaping from it, you are not trying to withdraw from it. In that there is no association; it is actual pain like having a toothache. It is pain. Can you be aware of it? Is there an awareness of it? Awareness of what actually is—pain. Now, in that is there dissociation?

'What do you mean?'

Wanting to get rid of it, wanting to run away from it.

'There would be if I didn't stay with it.'

Now, how are you staying with it? Are you forcing it? Are you trying to say, 'I must stay with it'?

'It ebbs as you talk because I am trying to answer you and it's very hard. It's a fluid thing. There is an impact and it flows through the mind and the system, as it were, and then it flows away.'

So there is a dissociation.

'But I do not feel that it is an action to get away. It's just like sound: the thunder fades away. You hear the impact and it disappears.'

Now, when you say that fragment is painful, that is actually what is. Keep to that. That is actually what is.

'Yes.'

Then what happens?

'If I stay with it and don't escape...'

No, don't say, 'If I stay with it.' Put away all those thoughts.

'It fades.'

Why has it faded?

'I think because the mind withdraws from it, unconsciously.'

Which means what?

'The mind reacts, as from the body, with a recoil from the intensity.'

That means the mind doesn't associate itself with the pain. Is that what you are saying?

'I think the mind becomes insensitive.'

Insensitive? To pain?

'Yes. It withdraws itself.'

Watch it! Therefore it dissociates itself from it. Therefore the mind becomes the observer pushing it away, or trying to forget it, or withdrawing.

'Then what does one do?'

What does the mind do with the fragment when it is aware that it is painful?

'The mind in a self-protective way changes fragments. The fragment that was pain now becomes the withdrawal from pain.'

That is the whole point. As long as there is a withdrawal, as long as there is the observer different from the thing observed, then pain, contradiction and conflict will exist. See the truth of this, that division will inevitably cause pain. And you saw the truth of it by being aware of actually what is.

'I don't think I did see the truth of it because I did exactly what the mind does.'

Therefore it is caught in the old habit.

'Yes. So I am not aware of it, if presumably awareness ends it.'

See this, see this. Become aware how the mind dissociates itself from the thing which it calls painful. But if it was pleasurable it wouldn't dissociate.

'Yes it would.'

It would? Why?

'Because the mind doesn't sustain any one thing, the mind moves from one thing to another.'

That's just it. Move, find out, be aware. Look what is happening, watch it. We said observe: observe a fragment, not the totality or the many fragments, just one fragment. When you became aware of that fragment it was painful. That is what actually is. Then the mind becomes weary of it, tired, withdraws, dissociates, becomes the observer and moves away from it. This is the habit of the mind. Now be aware of that habit, not of the pain. Be aware of this habit of withdrawing, whether it is from pleasure, pain, fear, whatever—withdrawing.

'But why did I withdraw if I really was aware of this *what is*?'

Because you were not aware. We said awareness implies remaining with it, watching it, watching the whole movement.

'But the whole movement was away.'

Watch that! Watch that movement away from it.

'But that's an evasion, that's thought, that's a duality.'

It doesn't matter, that's good enough. When you move away from pain, what is is the movement away.

'But then so is everything else that comes into my mind.'

Wait, go slowly. Watch, and therefore you see that what is *is a constant movement. You are missing the point.*

'Yes I am.'

Please just listen now. Don't say, 'I don't see.' Just watch it. We said be aware. And you said you were aware of one fragment which gives pain. I said to be aware of that pain, watch it. Then the mind moves away from it. The moving away from it is what is, *and it moves away to something else. So you are watching the movement—not to something. So* what is *is the movement. That movement is not pain or pleasure or association with something.*

'It *is* association with something. It is that chain. It goes back to that chain.'

Wait, I am coming to that. This means your movement is in the direction of association. It is only a movement in relation to something already fixed.

'One association begets another, yes. That's the chain.'

That is the chain. So we said be aware of one link of this chain entirely, be with it, watch it. Watch how the mind is incapable of observation completely without moving away from it. There are only two things, the movement away and what is.

'They are the same thing in me.'

So what does that mean? You see, it reveals that the mind is never quiet. It moves from association to association. It is never quiet with the one fragment, with one link. It is caught in the movement of association, which is a process, which is mechanical. And therefore there is despair that it can never end. And therefore we accept things as they are. And therefore it becomes the dead weight of the past.

Now, the mind observing that one fragment, which is pain, if it is not caught in the movement of association it observes with absolute quietness, as you observe that flower. Absolutely quietly. In that quiet observation there is no observer and therefore no movement of association. It is the observer who separates himself from the thing observed that is caught in the movement of association. All this is part of awareness—to observe, to be aware of the fragment and to be aware how restless the mind is through association, and to be aware of that restlessness. To be completely aware of that restlessness. To be aware of that restlessness so completely is possible only when the mind is really quiet to observe.

'But if the mind is restless, it's not quiet.'

No. You got away from it again. The mind is restless because it has not understood the movement of association, not seen the truth or the falseness of this movement of association. If you see that, see the truth of how endless this mechanistic process of association is, then the very observation of that truth ends the association. Because you don't see it, it goes on with the mechanistic habit.

51

THE STRANGE SENSE OF OTHERNESS

A curious thing happened the other day. It had been raining for many days, with a strong wind. The wind was blowing from the north-west and was quite cold though it was late spring. Many trees were still bare and the fields were not yet bright green for there hadn't been sun for many, many days. You got wet as you walked in the field but there was beauty—all the trees, the distant view and the sodden earth. You walked ahead with the dog. Among the trees suddenly that strange sense of otherness was there. That quality of otherness seemed to precipitate itself on the earth and in one's mind. All that evening it pursued you. You didn't invite it, you didn't even think about it. It came in the fullness of great beauty and an extraordinary sense of joy. The man might be considered well read. He had travelled a great deal and seen many so-called important people. He was telling us of the different political situations in the world, expanding on the wars, the pollution, and the friendship that he was trying to cultivate between two countries. Almost unknowingly he said, 'There is this world and the other. There is this world of everyday life and misery, and the other of liberation, moksha, nirvana, heaven, whatever you like to call it.'

It struck afterwards how we have divided this world and the world that is indescribable, that cannot be put into words. This division exists in every religion. This is the traditional approach, the traditional attitude, well established, deeply rooted in the mind of man. Really the two are indivisible; they are one. Yet we try to establish order in this world without the other. Without the other, thought cannot bring about the desired peace, a totally different way of living. Without the other, matter becomes very important. Thought is matter.

A blackbird was on the lawn near the wet tree. Across the field a large rabbit was sitting, its back to the house, its head held high, looking into the distance.

The movement of thought, however refined, is not the other.

52

MEDITATION IS TO SEE THE FACT OF DISTORTION

Meditation is not an escape from life; quite the contrary. The total understanding of the whole complex process of living from day to day with all its variations, pressures and strains is part of meditation. To observe what we are doing, our thoughts, our deep inward activities, without any distortion is part of this meditation. It is distortion that brings conflict in life. It is distortion that makes for separation, for brutality and violence. It is distortion that brings about aggression, competition and the continuous craving for pleasure. It is distortion that prevents the mind from seeing exactly *what is*. To observe without distortion, not only the external happenings but the inward movement of thought and motives, is part of meditation. There is distortion when there is the observer. The observer is the whole content of consciousness. It is this content that divides. This content is the factor of distortion because it is conditioned. This conditioning is belief, opinion, personal attitudes and temperament.

Meditation is the understanding of all this, for if this is not completely understood, distortion will remain, and so illusion. It is the distorted mind that gets caught in the many varieties of pleasurable happenings and entertainments, whether they are religious or secular. Meditation is to observe this fact of distortion and all its complicated ramifications. If this distorting factor is not wholly understood—not at the verbal level but at a non-verbal and therefore much deeper level—meditation becomes a form of self-hypnosis and hysterical activity which has absolutely nothing to do with reality.

In meditation the observer totally disappears and so therefore does the entity that craves for experience, and the brain that records and experiences; the wider and deeper aspects of meditation are when the observer is not, and the recording in the brain cells does not take place. It is recording that gives a continuity to the observer who is the factor of distortion. To observe without the observer is to observe with the totality of the mind in which the brain is wholly quiet. It is the function of the brain to record. On this recording its safety depends, its security, its self-centred activity. When this function does not operate, the brain functions most efficiently and sanely. It is the self-centred activity that is everlastingly seeking security in both the rational and the irrational, in the fact and non-fact. This sustains the resistance of the self, the 'me' and the 'not-me'. Meditation is the intelligence that is aware of the movement of the self.

This awareness brings out without any effort all the motives, the will, the drive of the hidden movements of the self. This intelligence does not suppress or cover up the subtle activities of the observer as the self. This intelligence, being free, opens the door to expose the content of consciousness which is consciousness itself.

Knowledge is not creative. The recording machinery of the brain is knowledge and thought uses that knowledge as a means of security. This security has its roots in the past; the security of tomorrow is the momentum of the past. Meditation is to be aware of this in daily life, and only then does the observer cease to be a distorting factor. In meditation there is no recording so each movement of meditation is new and different. It is never repetitive. There is in it something new and inexpressible. This is meditation.

53

WE DON'T SEE THE WHOLE

Meditation is not a personal adventure to some pleasurable unknown. The content of consciousness is consciousness; the content and consciousness are not separate. The content is the whole of the person: the ego, the characteristics, the tendencies and idiosyncrasies, the temperament and character. All this is the content; this is the structure of consciousness with its various fragmentations, the higher and the lower, the will, the resistance, the submission, the comparison and conformity. The personal adventure that one seeks in meditation through experience is the conditioned response of the content of consciousness. The pleasure principle is the main drive of consciousness. Meditation is the total denial of the content. This may appear as self-destruction; and it is. Willing consciousness is the becoming of pleasure, and the other side of the coin is fear and pain. The content of consciousness is the known, though that known may be hidden; the content is not only the great accumulation of knowledge as tradition but also the unresolved problems and the attachment to the repetitive scenes and images of pleasure and pain that have been stored up. These come to the surface; their appearance may be temporary and can be pushed aside for the time being but they will recur over and over again because of the need of an inattentive mind to be occupied. All knowledge is the known and consciousness can function only in this field.

The understanding of these adventures and hopes is also meditation. The known and the unknown lie close together and the harmony between the two is intelligence. The more there is understanding of the known the more there is freedom from it. The understanding of the known, which is the self, the content of consciousness with its will and effort, forces oneself to be watchful. It only sees the surface mode but when there is free observation without any motive, the hidden contents of consciousness are exposed naturally. One can study these exposures, learn about them and so be free of them. But if there is an intention or motive to be free of them or an intention to study them you are merely observing the surface movement and not the total movement. The art of learning about oneself is to come upon oneself casually, freely. If you have motive, your motive destroys your study because your motive is a dead thing.

We don't see the whole, we see only fragments, because our minds are fragmented. That is a fact. Our minds are fragmented because we observe through image of the 'me' or the 'not me', which inevitably breaks up light. See light as a whole and look.

54

MEDITATION IS THE MOVEMENT OF GREAT SENSITIVITY

It was a Sunday morning with clear blue sky. The sun was on the palm trees and the magnolia and you could hear church bells ringing. The bells of Rome have an extraordinary sound; no other church bells in the world have that peculiar quality and tonality. They began very early this morning in the distance and the nearby church took up with its own bells. The whole city began to fill with this strange sound of deep bells. One could ride on these sounds, go far away. After all, the repetition of words, of mantras, does produce a peculiar sound inwardly.

Meditation is not provoked by sound. It is not a thing that you decide upon. It is not a thing that you practise day after day in a quiet spot, sitting with eyes closed. It is not the control of the movement of thought. It is not adjustment to the pattern which the mind has set, nor is it a discipline forced by circumstances or by one's own volition. You can ride very far away on the sound of a bell or on the sound of your own voice or the sound of a bird in the trees, but this in no way clears the mind and the heart to see, it in no way makes the body or the mind sensitive.

Meditation is the movement of great sensitivity, for sensitivity is the highest form of intelligence. When there is this clear, simple, intense sensitivity and intelligence then mediation has quite a different meaning.

It is strange how human beings give so many different meanings to meditation. There are schools of various kinds that teach meditation. There are various teachers with their own peculiar forms of meditation; each guru has his own system dependent on the conditioning of the teacher, the guru and the many inventors of forms of meditation. But true meditation is freeing the mind from all conditioning and thereby laying the foundation of righteous behaviour and action. It is emptying the mind of the past and the hurt of all the wounds, miseries, conflicts and sorrow. This is part of right and true meditation. For this no guru, no teacher, no system is necessary. On the contrary, the teacher, the guru, the system, become a burden. By their very nature and structure, they prevent the perception of what is true.

Meditation is the setting aside of all the conditioning which has been imposed on the mind for centuries and freeing the heart of all the wounds of many years. Then only one begins to understand the true nature of meditation.

This brings about innocency. Innocency means to be utterly incapable of being wounded. Innocency means to have no resistance of any kind. This innocency is destroyed when there is will, desire and the pleasure that comes about when the mind is a slave to the verb *to be*. 'To be' is to have; 'to be' has conditioned the mind; the word itself has forced the mind and the brain to conform to the pattern set by the word. Meditation is freeing the mind of the past and the future, and this is not possible when the mind is caught in the verb *to be*— that is, when there is the emphasis of the 'I am' or the rule of the past over the present, which shapes the future. All this is the outcome of the word and the verb *to be*, which establishes the 'I am'. When there is 'I am' there is no meditation.

Time is yesterday, today and tomorrow; the infinite past, the insistent present and the limited future. The mind and the brain are slaves to time. Freeing of the mind from time is part of meditation; to free the mind not only of yesterday but of the many thousand yesterdays. The tradition, the memory, the experience, the knowledge—whether racial, of the family or of one's own gathering—all that is the past which in response to the present is modified and so projects the shadow of the future. This conditions the mind.

In meditation, being aware of the whole content of one's brain and mind and observing it very closely without any evaluation, judgement or condemnation, just observing, brings freedom. It is only when there is this freedom in meditation that the mind becomes very clear, not corrupted by the past or by the present. To such a mind there is no future, for the future is the movement of the 'I am' which will have something to gain or to lose in the future.

When the mind has understood deeply at all the levels of its own being then there is the clarification of the heart. Then there is love. So meditation is the emptying of the mind of the past and the future and of all the wounds and the aching memories and pleasures of the heart. Out of this meditation comes a deep silence. Only then can *that which is* be seen.

55

CAN THE BRAIN EVER BE QUIET?

We do not seem to be aware of the psychological structure of the brain. Most of us carry on mechanically in the condition in which we are born and educated, living a repetitive life, with certain modifications. We are trained from childhood until we die to function within a very small part of our brain's capacity, whether we are scientists, engineers or anything else. A scholar, a priest, a theologian or a politician functions within a very small fragment of the brain. We all use that part of the brain which is always of yesterday. All specialisation is exclusive and fragmentary, limited and narrow. All this is the old brain which is the result of millions of years of struggle for survival, struggle to get the best out of the environment, and so on. This is all we know and with this brain we try to explore and discover something new. Therefore there is always deep-rooted frustration and despair.

This old brain is memory and memory is always fragmentary. Every challenge—which must be new if it is a challenge at all—is met by the old brain responding according to its old patterns. Being aware choicelessly of this process, the brain itself understands its own nature and structure, and so only responds in a mechanical way to mechanical demands like writing, spelling and so on. Obviously this mechanical part of the brain must function where memory is involved. But when we make a challenge out of something which is not a challenge, like meeting someone who insulted us or flattered us some time ago, this is a mechanical response which is habitual. This response is unnecessary and without it there would be no challenge at all! So what we generally consider to be challenges are simply mechanical responses to events.

This is the way we live. All these responses are from what we call the old brain. Is the *whole* operation of the brain old? Is there any action of the brain which is not this response of the computer? And can this brain ever be quiet? Can it be active when it is demanded and silent when it is necessary? The answer to this lies in meditation. The understanding of this mechanical habitual brain opens the door to the new quality of the mind. When we say *the new* we mean something entirely different, a different dimension which cannot possibly be formulated by the old. Anything that can be formulated by the old brain is not new, for this very formulation is the action of memory which is image and thought. When the new is very close to the old, the old can reach it, touch it and contaminate it. But if the new is very far from the old then the old cannot reach it. Thought can be quiet and produce a certain silence which is the cessation of its own chattering. But this silence with its space around a centre is not the new. The new is not just the cessation of the old.

The old brain must be ready to operate mechanically when it is needed, so it must not be asleep, anaesthetised, controlled, drilled; it must operate efficiently. To operate efficiently, every form of conclusion, judgement and justification must come to an end. When the old brain operates in the field of psychological prejudices, it ceases to be efficient, sane and rational. For the old brain to function so efficiently, so truly, it must be quiet. So there *is* the quietness of the old brain, which is not sleep, which is not a mythical, mystical state of induced vagueness. The new can be only when the old has completely understood its place and function. So our concern is not with the new, but having seen the whole nature and structure of the old then action is different. All our action is relationship. This different action of relationship is love, which is not the known. And meditation is freeing the mind from the known.

The separation between the old brain and the new can be perceived very definitely when the old brain loses its observer. The new cannot be perceived as the observer if the old brain sees the observed separate from itself. When the whole mechanism of the old with its observer becomes entirely quiet, keeps its acuity and therefore loses its observer, then the new is.

In a certain manner of speaking it is wrong even to make a division between the old and the new: they live in the same house, there is harmony between the two. This harmony cannot possibly exist without love. And meditation is of this love.

56

LOVE IS NOT AN ABSTRACTION

The mystery of meditation is not at the end but at the beginning. We have made it so difficult, so complex, something that has to be constantly practised, fought with or against, demanding a great deal of discipline, training. Meditation becomes very simple when you know what love is. Love is not an abstraction, a thing that has to be thought out, cultivated and guarded. To know love without mentation is really the problem. The thought that says, 'He has been good to me,' or insulted me or hurt me, is the mentation that prevents the innocency of love.

Man equates love with sex, with the family and the extension of that as the community, the nation and so on. So we put love into the framework of sex or into the religious design and thus we destroy it. Love includes all things but if you put it into the structure of thought you destroy it.

Man's life is institutionalised, organised, formalised into political and social patterns that enslave him. To break those patterns is revolution but that only creates other patterns which again enslave him. There seems no way out of this mounting complexity. Man's relationship to man cannot be solved through institutions; the further we go along those lines the more hopeless the confusion. This organisational approach to life must inevitably deny the inward life of man or entirely disregard it, for this evaluation of life divides the inner from the outer and hence there is a conflict between the two. But if we could approach life from the inner to the outer there would be no such division; then there would be only one movement. Aggression, violence and desire for power bring about their opposites, as non-aggression, non-violence, humility, kindness and so on, but all this has nothing to do with love. Our concern must be with love and not with institutions and bureaucracies. This concern is meditation.

MEDITATION IS EMPTYING
THE MIND OF WORD AND SYMBOL

Meditation is emptying the mind of word and symbol. A symbol is never the real, the word never the actual. What cannot be expressed in the word seems unreal but the word is not the expression of the real. What can be expressed, whether eloquently or stupidly, is not the actual.

To live on words is to live in separation and hence in the conflict of duality. To live without words is to see the movement of the whole. The symbol has become more urgent and meaningful than the fact. The philosophy of the word is the love of the surface of the common mind. It is the symbol that is worshipped and adored in the church and the temple; and even when, as in the mosque, there is no outward symbol the word takes its place. Thought in its search for the divine inevitably makes it into a symbol or a word, and the whole conditioning of the mind begins.

The word divides and in that division thought lives. The life of thought has become more meaningful than the actual life, for the mind has become the slave of the word. For the linguistic philosopher or scientist the structure of words is far more significant than the mind that is empty of the word. The label has become more important than the man behind the label; and the man himself is made up of words and symbols—the 'me' is the remembrance of the past in image and form. This form is within the framework of thought as memory. To the linguistic scientist the world is filled with thought, the structure of the word and its communication; and what is communicated is of little meaning. It is like the analyst who hopes to cure the patient so that he can go back into a corrupt society.

Love is not memory nor the word. It may be expressed in word, in gesture or in act, but the gesture, the word or the act are not love. When love is put into the frame of thought it becomes pleasure, the desire for which is sustained by the image.

The brain cells hold the matter of thought and thought is as material as the carpet under a chair. Is there thought without the word? And without thought, what is the mind? Thought is the burned remains of yesterday, and the ashes cover the mind. To burn away those ashes in the fire of the present is to empty the mind of the word and the symbol. Meditation is seeing instantly this whole movement of the word. The seeing is the doing. The doing is postponed when the word interferes with the seeing. In the interval between the seeing and the doing is the whole misery of man.

THE ENDING OF TIME IS
THE ENDING OF CHANGE

The ending of time is the ending of change. Being, trying to become, invents time. Being, whatever it be, is without time. The word is of time and when the word is associated with being, the illusion of movement from this to that takes place. Being undergoes a radical transformation when the mind is free of time. The probing into this is meditation. To probe is not to achieve. If you probe deliberately with intention of discovery then what you discover will be the projection of your past. If you probe without 'you', the thinker, then probing is inexhaustible. The intention to probe comes with the intention to find, but the finding becomes trivial when it is an experience. Experience is recognition and recognition is association, the past. There must be the abandonment of what is discovered in probing, all the time, for this allows freedom. Without freedom inquiry is negated.

The constant is of no-time but it is not stationary. Meditation is the freeing from that state of mind that possessing decays. Innocency is this freedom. Love which possesses destroys itself. Meditation is the throwing away of all man's cunning and the throwing away of the morality of thought.

The wood was very thick, full of spring leaves, and as you looked through them at the blue sky you could almost see every vein of the leaf. On the road that went by the wood the cars whizzed by and the wood remained stately, isolated and quiet. There were not many birds but a blackbird was sitting on a branch calling to its neighbour. The ground was thick with the leaves of many years and it was soft underfoot. The smell of decaying leaves and the smell of new leaves filled the air. It was an isolated spot, full of charm and beauty. Thought could not touch it but the senses were everywhere.

59

THOUGHT CANNOT EMPTY THE MIND

It had been foggy for several days. The hills were covered but you could just manage to see the outlines and the deepening curves of the valleys. Lupins and mustard were in full bloom, yellow, flowing like vast streams over the hills. The blue sea was as calm and still as a deep lake with hills around it. Not a breath stirred the leaves. It was an extraordinarily quiet morning. There were hundreds of birds—doves, quail, blue jays, mockingbirds and the ever-busy sparrows. They chattered away, playful, the males attacking each other. Two doves that came so silently after all the others had left were picking the grains that had been scattered for them all. The quail walked in a long row along the wall, one after the other on parade. They would fly off when they reached the end of the wall and disappear into the canyon.

At night there was a deep-throated owl, big, dark, sitting alone on the branch of a tree, hooting. As you watched, it flew away silently. Late at night towards the early morning it was hooting but its mate did not answer. They must have been on the roof or on the chimney. You heard them very close but to go out would disturb them so you remained in the room.

As morning came the hills were still in fog, the yellowing flowers in the deep canyons. The sea was as calm as ever, without a ripple. On the lawn where the grain was scattered there were about forty quail, the males with their long tufts over their heads, all hungry and pecking away. Their scratching of the earth was a dance; they would remain there for ten or fifteen minutes and suddenly take flight and disappear among the bushes, coming back again late in the afternoon.

There is something lovely in a foggy day when there is not a breath of air, when everything is still. At night, as one lay awake listening to the stillness, the mad destructive world seemed so far away—the violence, the postures, the many masks that human beings put on. Beyond the hills was lasting darkness but here in this quiet room life seemed endless, full of happiness, and so there was a benediction. When thought is the factor of decision in meditation then meditation is time-binding, superficial, visionary and shadowy. In the shadows there are many things unreal, for the shadow itself is unreal. Thought can never listen and can never see. Thought does not have the extreme sensitivity of seeing and listening. Thought by its very nature is dull, for it has its roots in the past. When thought decides to control, to meditate, to change, to create a new structure of society, its very movement is a distortion. As our minds are filled with the things of thought, images and symbols, words and conclusions, our eyes and ears become dull, insensitive. It is part of meditation to see and listen without any distortion.

There is no magical power in frustration, in the tortuous ways of thought. Meditation is the emptying of the mind of all symbols, words and sorrows. Thought cannot empty the mind. The decision to empty the mind is to invite frustration and endless means and efforts. Thought has made the organism of the body dull, merely sensuous, coarse and sluggish. The body itself is not lazy; it is thought that makes the body lazy. Thought becoming aware of the laziness then strives hard to drive it, push it out of bed. Thought is indolent in its outlook, indolent in its movements and is comfort-seeking, so the body becomes insensitive. When the body is made insensitive by thought, the mind and the heart follow the easy movement of deterioration.

All this is time-binding. Meditation is to be aware of all this without the choice of thought. Then you will see that hearing and seeing become naturally subtle and swift. For the mind must be swift and subtle, not with the subtlety of cunningness which is part of thought but with the swiftness of the breeze on the hills, which leaves no mark, no memory. Then the mind is free of time and experience. And forever the first step is the last step.

60

SILENCE

On the high plateau surrounded by snow-capped mountains is a solitary tree, very large, with a great trunk and wide-spreading branches full of leaves and deep shadows. It must be very old. A storm must have destroyed the other trees around it, for you saw stumps broken off and covered with moss, lichen and edelweiss. It was really extraordinary to see that tree against the blue sky of the spring, so clear, distant and completely alone. The plateau was large and by it flowed a stream, gurgling down the steep hill into the valley far below. That tree had no companion, no one to whisper to it. Its branches did not wave, dance in the breeze with others. It was very strangely alone, had lived many years, and there it stood in solitary majesty. Every morning you saw it, in spite of the rain and occasional fog. You saw it in the evening light when all the other trees were in shadow. There it was, lit by the setting sun. It was far more majestic than the mountains, the rocks and the solitary hut.

It attracted your eye—not only your eye but your heart, for it conveyed to you its solitude, its sense of aloofness from the world, its quiet, great dignity, and you had to look. It was the first thing you looked at when you got up. You drew the curtain and there it was, full of life, with a great sense of beauty. It was really quite extraordinary to see and you watched it for a very long time. There was communion between you and it. You didn't know what this communion meant but there it was, timeless, spaceless, in that great solitude. The solitude was not only of the tree but the solitude that one has in oneself. Not aching loneliness, not the weary burden of having no companion, but the solitude of immense silence. Perhaps not *immense* because that silence you could not measure. It defied all measurement, all comparison.

It is strange how in the solitude of silence in which there is no awareness of its own existence, there is a quality of no-time. Silence is always alone. This silence is not the cessation of noise; it has quite a different quality and a different dimension. It is not that you can force or train yourself to be silent. If you do that, it has quite a different quality, a different feel, a different action altogether. The silence that is produced by the mind in its desire to bring about a withdrawal from worldly affairs, from the chaos and confusion and from one's own strife and misery has a very limited and narrow space. That silence is never free. That silence is always held within many walls.

The silence that was there that morning as you looked at that marvellous tree was entirely different. It was not the opposite of noise, though cars were coming up the hill and the lorry was changing its gears. That noise was there but it had no relationship with the silence that was between. It was not *between* you and the tree but was simply there. And you remained. Not as a watcher. You were not even there. If you were there the silence would not have been and the tree would be just a tree like so many others. But because you weren't there the silence was there. And as you turned away from the window to carry on with what you had to do, that silence was moving into thought and action.

The human mind is never alone. It has so many experiences, is burdened with so many words, the memories of so many things stored deep within itself, the impressions, the conclusions, the opinions, the propaganda that has been put into the mind. It carries it wherever it goes—on a walk, in the air, sitting quietly, ruminating about things, or in the solitary cell of the prisoner or the monk. It is never alone. And the mind that is alone...

To empty the heart of the things of the mind and the things of bodily responses is solitude. Love alone can live in solitude without distortion.

Made in the USA
Monee, IL
03 May 2026